Pear Shaped

ISBN: 978-1-51186-061-1
Cover: Susanne Worsfold and Carl Stockley

First published in paperback in 2015

Pear Shaped

ADAM BLAIN

About the Author

Adam Blain was born in London in 1970, the youngest of three brothers. Having studied law at Cambridge, Adam spent time working as a teacher in Lesotho, Southern Africa before returning to practice corporate law in London. Following diagnosis of a grade 4 glioblastoma multiforme (GBM) brain tumour in 2014, Adam wrote his first book, *Pear Shaped*. Adam continues to live in London with his wife and three children and remains working as a corporate lawyer.

You can follow Adam and his progress on Twitter:
@AdamBBlain

For my wonderful wife Lu and my three adorable children, all of whom make me laugh and make life worth fighting for. This is also dedicated to my fellow GBM sufferers - may you all be one of the lucky ones.

Preface

I'm just a normal kind of bloke. There are some people I know who are genuinely nice, decent and thoroughly good people. The kind of people who, if you believe in Heaven, will walk straight in, no questions asked. OK, they may have to flash some ID but their place in Heaven is guaranteed and obvious. Well, unfortunately I am not like that. But I'm not a bastard either. Nearly everyone who knows me would place me in the range somewhere between "a pretty decent bloke" and "oh, that tosser". So I am boringly mid-range. People don't flock to me in their hundreds nor do they avoid me. I am reasonably clever and (I think) good at my job as a corporate lawyer. I am staunchly middle-class, have a lovely wife, three kids and great friends and extended family. Boring stuff. In fact when I digest my entire personality and achievements into a single opening paragraph, I admittedly come across as a bit dull. However, I am not dull if for no other reason than the fact that I have a rare and interesting disease. Another reason I am not dull (or not that dull) is that I have several unusual superpowers. I do not like to boast but I believe they have some relevance to my story.

Here's how it all began…….

Diagnosis Day

It is Spring 2014. I'd been under the weather and suffering from headaches and this really weird thing I called "Sicky Vom Gobby Splat". For no apparent reason, several times in the day, I'd start to feel nauseous and my saliva glands would go into warp-drive. I'd then eject mouthful after mouthful of saliva for a couple of minutes until it passed. This always seemed to happen on the way through Warren Street station – explain that one then, medics! I'd also been having terrible headaches. My wife, Lu (who happens to be an oncologist) insisted I went to get a scan just to "rule out anything nasty". Well that was the plan.

I pitched up at A&E as a fit-looking bloke in his mid-forties complaining of headaches. You could almost read the thoughts of the triage nurse:

"I hope you have a good long book and plenty of money for the vending machine. You're going to be here longer than the drinking-water dispenser and that's got another seven months to run on its contract."

You can imagine the conversation with the doctor:

"You have what we call a 'moderately bad headache'. We treat this with a drug called 'Paracetamol' – you may have heard of this. Your complaint can be exacerbated by loud noise, heavy drinking or banging your head. It's nothing to worry about – moderately bad headaches are quite common and they don't kill you over a period of months."

But no – this was the parallel universe that (unfortunately) wasn't to be.

Instead, I was being pushed around the hospital in a wheelchair by someone in their mid-fifties who looked in worse shape than me. You know it's going to be bad when the NHS won't let you move to the next appointment under your own steam. It would have been so much more reassuring if they said:

"Here are your roller blades. Whizz down to the MRI scanner. Careful on the stairs!"

There was another way I could tell how bleak my situation was. My first hospital was the North Middlesex in Edmonton. Lu works at this hospital so she knows many of the doctors, and these doctors kept buying me coffees. Not cheap canteen coffee but expensive coffee shop lattes. Since when did NHS doctors have the time or money to buy patients a four quid coffee? Whilst I did not want to sound ungrateful, this could not be a good sign.

To top it all off, I was then moved from North Middlesex Hospital to Queen Square Hospital by ambulance. Ambulance! Now I really knew I was in trouble. In fact, ambulance is the third worst means of transport from this perspective, only beaten by air ambulance and hearse. I am only counting for these purposes means of transport that are plausible. So I exclude being rolled down the road in a large industrial steel drum labelled "Fresh Body Parts, not suitable for transplantation".

Two scans and two hospitals later the same day, I was jotting down the guest list to my funeral:

"What's he ever invited me to?" and

"He can go on the B List, and so can pitch up only if one of the A Listers can't make it or isn't crying hard enough."

That said, even this early on, I was determined to have a positive funeral where my life is celebrated. Possibly even a photographer:

"Smile everyone. We'll have the deceased's family and friends on this side and the widow's family and friends over there. Now let's have a photo of the deceased's university friends and next one of his ex-girlfriends; then we'll have a photo of the lucky one who catches the wreath. Finally we'll have a photo of the beautiful new widow. Doesn't she look a picture of elegance in her outfit made of torn, black sacking?"

You never know how you are going to react to really terrible news about yourself. Straight after the diagnosis was actually not the most chaotic point. At that moment in time I was mostly open-mouthed, gawping into space with doing that kind of comedy slow blinking. I was then expected to immediately start absorbing information about my diagnosis.

Apparently there are different grades of cancer. Mine is grade 4, which is the worst you can get. So it's the opposite to competency in music, and the higher the grade, the worse news it is. It also means that medical staff explain things to you with a kind of wince etched on their face as if to make the point. I have what's called a Glioblastoma Multiforme (GBM), which is Latin for "I hope you've got your will sorted and affairs in order".

Just the words themselves are so damning: "brain cancer". You do not need to be medically qualified in any way to understand this. You take the worst and most incurable disease there is. Apply this to the most important organ in your body - the part you would least like diseased or fiddled around with.

Again:

BRAIN CANCER

Those two words just portray absolute horror and despair without the need for any medical interpretation. It is a bit like being told you have "testicle rupture" - it is never going to be good news. You do not need a doctor or other medic to tell you this. Of course there will be the optimists constantly looking for that silver lining. They would claim that:

"At least with your diagnosis of testicle rupture, both words were in the singular, when either or both could be plural (allowing for grammar). It could be much worse. Look on the bright side!"

I try to avoid these people and find that such ultra-optimists are suffering from "personality annoying".

At times of crisis like this I found it is best to focus on the trivial. For example, every time a nurse or doctor saw me they produced a few of these giant cotton buds. One went up each nostril and one in the crease of my groin. It turns out they were testing for MRSA – this bacteria obviously liking the least pleasant places in my body. If they needed more tests, I could think of at least two more unpleasant places where they could stick those things. In fact I may have three, although in one case I suspect that even MRSA would not want to live there.

What was odd was the number of times this happened – every time I saw a member of staff it's cotton-bud time. "Hello, Mr Blain, I'm Doctor X" – and out come the cotton buds. It was a bit like a strange alien greeting used instead of a handshake. I spent a lot of my time looking like some large novelty toiletry dispenser.

It has crossed my mind that this may have all been based on an original prank by junior doctors that got out of hand, and which had now taken on a life of its own.

A couple of days previously I was walking around Finchley with an annoying headache. This had rapidly changed to hospitalisation and me fighting for my life. In a situation such as this a person has two main pillars of support, namely friends and family. In both regards I have done extremely well. If you are going to have your life fall apart around you and die prematurely, you may as well do it in style and accompanied on the journey by thoroughly decent and caring people.

So when you have news like this dumped on you without warning what you really need is three university friends to take you out for a burger.

Let me tell you a little about my inner circle of friends – basically we are four blokes from university: Gary, Kim (yes, apparently it can be a male name), Carl and myself. When we get together our topics of conversation include:

1) Our various indiscretions at university with members of the opposite sex, particularly where the act in question (or, in some cases, omission):
    i) did not go to plan,
    ii) did not happen at all or
    iii) kind of happened and did so roughly according to plan but in the wrong direction.

2) Our bowel movements.

3) The order in which we are going to die.

Actually, by "include" I mean "consist entirely of ". We have exactly the same conversations every time we meet. And yet far from being boring, this is strangely reassuring, especially for conversation 3) where I am Number Three out of four. It's not like a competition between us – it is just us interpreting fate. The important thing is to know who the one is before you so you know when to start eating spirolina and lay off the burgers a bit. I keep a close eye on Carl's medical condition as he is Number Two. Gary, rather unfairly, has been picked out as Number One although as you will see, he gets the last laugh (not that he will laugh – he will be terribly upset and left without a regular curry partner). Of all my friends, Gary is the one I see the most. I reckon in our lives we must have had over 500 curries together. Not enough in my opinion.

Now, back to the burger. Of course I had to go in my pyjamas (clothes hadn't found their way to me yet) with a variety of pipes and needles sticking out of my arm making me look like an easily distracted junkie. In spite of this, the quarter pounder and chocolate milkshake went down an absolute treat even if I was a little nervous that my handlers and I looked like something from a Little Britain sketch.

Immediately following diagnosis was a week of utter chaos. Not particularly sad, angry or morbid. If I could summarise my life in one word at this point in time it would be "Aaaaaggghhhhh!". Unfortunately nothing deep and meaningful or clever. I also became totally subsumed into the NHS. I was now part of the statistics on some Cabinet minister's desk.

Hospitalisation

It was only a matter of hours since diagnosis and I was already exasperated by how medicalised my life had become and how suddenly this had arisen. There were tubes going into me and out of me. Needles pumping stuff into me and taking blood out of me. Things constantly being monitored, pushed into me (and, ahem, up me). And every meal had an hors d'oeuvre of a pile of pills. My bedroom was a few square feet of lino surrounded by a curtain, constantly invaded by medical staff and I could not remember my last visitor who wasn't massaging white alcoholic foam into their hands or sticking something round my arm that inflates. Decisions such as whether I could wash my hair (what's left of it after my pre-operation shave) have been taken away as well as what shampoo I am allowed to use (only baby shampoo, if you are interested). I was not under the NHS – I was very much part of it and, as such, had lost control of my life.

I had been given three different types of anti-nausea meds. Each had a different degree of effectiveness and accompanying equivalent levels of constipation. The most potent is a drug that completely stops you throwing up or even feeling like you have that need, which is great so long as you had no plans to have a bowel movement that week. It is seriously constipating. So the active ingredient must be a drug that simply stops stuff departing the body.

Treatment

When I was transferred to Queen Square Hospital on diagnosis day, it was immediately clear to the doctors that I needed to have an operation. Like everyone else in the entire world (aside from the odd Münchausen syndrome sufferer) I do not like operations, at least when they are conducted on me. I have had a couple of moles chopped out of my back and a fairly neat umbilical hernia operation after I overdid the stomach crunches a bit in the gym one weekend. Those procedures were just a bit inconvenient. However, this head operation is serious as it is not just about stuff at skin level. To me it is a particularly bad operation because:

1) It involves not just cutting with a scalpel but also sawing bone. They actually have to break bone (and of course skin) before they can even start. They make a little hatch in the side of my head, like a trap door you would find as a way in to a cheap loft extension.

2) It must be a difficult operation as they needed someone as clever as a brain surgeon to do it.

3) There must be a serious risk that my Superpowers will be damaged or, even worse, lost completely.

Generally speaking I do not like things being chopped off or out of me. I have had things chopped off and out of me before, like the moles I mentioned – plus, I'm Jewish. However, of all the parts of you that you do not want bits chopped off, the brain must come in the top two.

Carl had an idea regarding the operation. Instead of putting the missing piece of skull back, they could put in a piece of glass or toughened transparent plastic, cut to size. This way my brain could be monitored without having to open me up. In fact, why not put some tropical fish in there to make a feature of it? I suppose they would have to operate on a daily basis in order to feed the fish with a big op each week to change the water and clean it all out. Carl does not always think his ideas through.

The operation is presented to you as a choice and they ask for your consent, in writing. I was asked if I wished to proceed with the operation. I asked what would happen if I said "no". Without any doubt I would die and do so soon. So the operation came strongly recommended. I therefore participated in all of this "voluntarily" in the same way that a mugging victim voluntarily hands over his wallet. If you will excuse the pun, for me the decision was a no-brainer.

Following the operation I was told I would have to undergo an ongoing programme of treatment of radiotherapy coupled with chemotherapy tablets. The theory was (and believe me, it is just a theory) that these two treatments work well in parallel and snuff out the odd cancerous cell that may have slipped past the surgeon. It is the best chance that the NHS can offer so there was no debate as to whether or not I proceed.

The Operation

So, just four days after being diagnosed, they sawed open half my skull and took out a lump of brain the size of a pear.

A PEAR!

That's how the surgeon described it. And the first question to enter my head: What sort of pear? A conference pear? A Bartlett, Anjou? Is there any significance in the shape? Was it actually pear-shaped?

If they are going to gauge the size by reference to fruit, why did it have to be something as big as a pear? Why not a grape or, if very unlucky, an apricot? If you stay out of melon and pineapple territory, a pear is actually one of the worst-sized fruits to be used as a comparator for the size of a piece of brain they chop out, being pretty big and ambiguous as a reference point. To be fair to the surgeon, the size is less ambiguous than it would be for, say, an apple, which varies in size from crabapple to bramley. Also if it had resembled a pineapple, aside from the sheer size of the thing, getting that knobbly shape all the way round would really take some skill on the part of the surgeon. In fact they would probably have to get in a chef from a Thai restaurant who does that thing where they carve carrots into strange shapes and you never know whether or not you are meant to eat them and, more importantly, how many other people's plates they have been on.

The operation itself is called a "de-bulking", where they cut out as much of the tumour as possible. I did not want an operation called "de-bulking". I wanted it called "removing", "eradicating" or (dare I say it) "curing". De-bulking sounds a bit half-hearted, like something you would hear from builders:

"We couldn't remove the mountain of rubbish we left in your garden but we did de-bulk it."

"Don't bloody de-bulk it. Go back, hire another skip and get rid of it!"

Or, if staying at a friend's house:

"I'm really sorry but when I used your toilet after that very heavy meat-based meal a blockage arose and it all backed up. I apologise for this. I haven't exactly resolved the problem but I can say quite confidently that I have taken steps to de-bulk it."

To which they reply:

"NO – that's not good enough! Roll up your sleeves and sort it. And for future reference there's that burger place five minutes down the road which you must now always use when you come to visit."

I was trying to imagine the operation, being very curious indeed about it (and you will see that this curiosity ultimately gets the better of me). Whenever I picture the operation in my head it is a bit different each time, although the ending is always the same. I always imagine it finishing with the surgeon lifting the chopped-out pear high into the air, whilst everyone else in the operating theatre drops to their knees in awe and then, in perfect unison, sing "Circle of Life" from *The Lion King.*

If you wear a white coat or one of those blue hospital orderly outfits, you don't call it a "pear" but instead use the term "right temporal lobe". I'll stick with "pear" as I don't want to be accused of showing off.

Apparently I had a right temporal lobectomy. Looking at it from Pear's perspective, it had a nearly-all-of-Adam-ectomy. This highlights an important philosophical point: Which part is actually "me", and how much do they have to chop off before the bit they dispose of is "me". Meanwhile "I" (i.e. the bit left) become mere surgical waste. Perhaps a medic can confirm, but from the hospital's perspective the "me" bit is the part that signs the discharge papers and to whom they say goodbye and good luck (without irony). If it leaves by a chute it does not count as "me".

I was plumbed into various bags and pipes for a number of days after the operation. I had a catheter, a drip and a "drain" to remove any excess brain fluid or whatever. I hoped they didn't get anything mixed up and in particular I hoped that one of the bags marked "out" did not get mixed up in the plumbing with a bag marked "in".

It was also a bit strange having a chat with a friend or family member, who had kindly given up their time to visit me, and right between us throughout the conversation was a bag of my wee. It somehow always found its way into any discussion. I would say:

"It is very hot and dry in this ward."

To which they would reply:

"Yes, I can see. That's the colour of puddle water and it hasn't gone drip for the last five minutes."

I found that maintaining dignity in hospital was difficult. It was a huge relief to have the catheter removed (and thank you to the nice nurse) but when it's yanked out, is it normal for your ears to go pop?

The Pear Effect

So what parts of my brain were present in "the pear" and therefore removed?

Top 10 parts of my brain I hoped haven't been removed:

1) Sarcasm.

2) Sense of perspective.

3) Irony.

4) Cynicism.

5) Ability to parallel park (I'm really good at this!).

6) Ability to take the piss (I'm really good at this too!).

7) Spatial awareness.

8) Any other kind of awareness.

9) Any other kind of space.
And of course,

10) My three Superpowers.

Parts of my brain that I wouldn't mind so much being removed:

1) The OCD bit that constantly queries whether or not I remembered to turn the oven off.

2) The bit of my brain that is twenty years too old and says really stupid things that are inappropriate for my age such as:

   "You just can't beat a really good cup of tea" or
   "I really like this car – its very easy to get in and out of."

3) Nearly forgot – the tumoury bit. This is the point of the operation after all.

The surgeon was not so upbeat about my statistics and he advised against buying Christmas cards several years in advance although he didn't get to the stage where I was advised against buying green bananas. It seems that part of my brain included in the pear was the bit that was programmed to tell the rest of my body: "I know! Let's live into my mid-eighties." This came as a bit of a blow to me particularly as I'm death number three in the "Order". What's more, how am I going to break this news to Gary and Carl, who are now well and truly buggered? However, I must also warn them as soon as possible before they take up sky-diving or whatever.

Assessment Day

A couple of days after the operation I had to sit down to do a neuro assessment. Basically, this is to assess my mental functions and "draw a base-line" for future assessments. I had to sit down with a neuro psychologist for an hour and run through all sorts of tests. I did wonder whether, on the other side of the hospital, someone was sitting down with my "lost pear" to see what it knew. Then we could establish how good my brain was by taking my pre-op brain and subtracting the functionality of the pear bit.

I think the timing of the assessment was not the best. I was tired, disorientated and still partly off my tits on opiates. Things got off to a very bad start when the Neuro pyschologist said:

"We need to establish whether or not your brain functions can be considered to fall within the normal range. We'll therefore be looking at cognitive functions, memory and, most importantly, behavioural patterns. Now before we start, why have you got a cotton bud wedged up each nostril and another one you are currently fishing out from your pants?"

My attempt to impress by being proactive had clearly backfired.

The tests were strange. The first one involved looking at a book of about 100 photos and saying, in each case, whether the person in question was smiling or not. The problem was that the people in question looked like a batch of weirdo university academics from the 1970s with nylon shirts, wispy hair and the most ambiguous expressions. It really did look like part of the report from Operation Yewtree. Is that guy smiling?

He could be; it could be a grimace or possibly even trapped wind. The answer "neutral" seemed to get me through without too many black marks. Anyway, they didn't know how good I was at recognising friendly facial expressions before my op. This would explain why I got into so many fights with people supposedly smiling at me.

Being assessed did not stop me wanting to know as much as possible about my operation and the obvious person to grill was my surgeon, who was very forthcoming. I therefore had various bizarre conversations with him, for example:

"You said you took out part of my brain the size of a pear!"

"The tissue removed was indeed the size of a medium bartlett, but it was tumour and not brain."

"Oh, so it wasn't a chunk of my brain you chopped out?"

"No, not actual brain."

"Are you sure?"

"Absolutely."

"So the bit you chopped out: what is it made of?"

"Brain cells."

"Whose brain cells?"

"Yours."

"And where was it located?"

"In your brain."

"And now it's out, I'm definitely more stupid than before?"

"We don't like the word 'stupid'."

"So to recap: you took something made of my brain out of my brain, and as a result I'm now more thick."

"We don't like the word 'thick' either."
"Are you smiling at me or is that a grimace?"
"Smiling – can't you tell?"
"No. Do you want a fight?"

Assisted Shower

There is no separate shower block in my hospital. Instead, every ward has one or two "Assisted Showers" – nowhere near as raunchy as it sounds. They are intended to be disabled-friendly but even for a person in a perfectly fit state, they are the most impossible showers to use. No wonder people need assistance. Anyone other than an octopus would need to be assisted. Let me tell you about its design. Firstly, start off with a room that is just a little bit too small with a door that is difficult to lock. Put a toilet in there to take up much of the valuable floor space. I do not understand this doubling up of showers and toilets. They serve completely different functions (or they are meant to!) and frequently a person could require the services of one device without the other. Meanwhile, unless that person has a very strong friendship with the other person in question, only one person at a time would use the shower/toilet rendering one always effectively unavailable and unused. That is really annoying and offends my natural leanings towards efficiency. It is a bit like those pepper grinders with a salt cellar in the top. You do not always have both salt and pepper together. One person may be having pizza (pepper only) whilst the other may have chips (salt only) – a perfectly plausible situation, and yet one of them must wait and let their food get cold, in fact both if they are polite enough to wait for each other. It takes a whole lot longer to shower than grind out some pepper or sprinkle salt. And possibly longer still to go to the toilet depending upon the "number".

Next problem: more valuable floor space is taken up with three giant bins. Three! And they are huge. One is for general refuse (mostly paper towels). One is for unsanitary items like used bandages. The third is the scariest. It has bright yellow signs on it warning of hazardous contents: Must be where they dump body parts or at least toenail clippings. I knocked on the lid and called out to see if Pear was in there. He wasn't, but I think some of his mates were.

However, the biggest problem is the lack of a bracket to hold the shower head, so showering must be conducted in a one-handed fashion. This must be why the shower admits to requiring assistance. Whatever the pay of NHS staff (and I am not getting political here) it must be cheaper to put up a bracket to hold the shower than to pay staff to assist. Finally, the soap: not a bar of soap or a nice easy to use dispenser on the wall where you just push a knob. Shower gel comes in tiny sachets that you must collect and take in with you. Little foil sachets which are very tough and which do not have that cutaway bit to start the tear. So the left hand holds the shower head pointing it away from your towel and clothes at all times and trying not to get the scary yellow bin wet in case bits flush through it. You also want it to go nowhere near the toilet or floor round the toilet otherwise semi-toilet flushings may run towards your feet requiring the opening and use of another sachet of gel. Right hand holds the shower gel sachet which you attempt to open with your teeth. Of the 0.75 ml of shower gel generously provided in a sachet (of which 0.5 ml comes out), you end up swallowing 0.3 ml and you lather up with the remaining 0.2 ml if my maths serves me correctly. Only now do you understand why the nurse gave you ten sachets. Why did she not give me a guillotine too, to open them? If you can manage all of this efficiently you should not be in hospital - you should have your own show at Covent Garden where you do all this and juggle with your flip flops on a unicycle at the same time. So it is the least user-friendly shower I have ever used. You actually do not get assistance (well I didn't) so "assisted" must mean "disabled-friendly". So why is it "disabled-friendly"? Because there are two small white bars attached to the wall - vertically. I was beginning to wonder if this experience was actually part of my assessments. To pass this test I simply had to enquire if I could have a bath instead.

More Tests

As part of my new role as a lab rat, I participated in various assessments with a view to being released back into the wild. I was set this batch of strange practical tests by the occupational and physiotherapy team – a group of these small, female, Australasian therapists in their blue hospital outfits. I had to:

1) Walk up a flight of stairs, unassisted.
2) Find my way to the nearby shopping centre on foot.
3) Find out the time of the evening showing of a film at the cinema in the shopping centre.
4) Go into a supermarket to establish the price of a pint of milk.
5) Go into a coffee shop to establish the price of a small hot chocolate.

All of this while being followed around by my team of therapists in their head-to-toe blue uniforms. It's a bit like a charity fund-raising event we had at Cambridge during Rag Week in my university days, where you could pay a sum of money (to charitable causes) to have someone followed for the whole day by all seven of Snow White's dwarves. Lectures, tutorials, bars and dates – your seven friends (in the full get-up) stuck to you like glue. Here I was with my half-dozen smurfs, tailing me (but close enough to catch me if I fall over) with their clipboards, making notes of my every move. I had to complete these tasks without being caught by the evil wizard Gargamel.

I was planning to take Lu out for a meal as soon as I got out of hospital. Do I now need to reserve a table for eight at our favourite Vietnamese restaurant? I don't know if it's like being accompanied by dogs: do smurfs have to be left tied to the railings outside? To be safe I'll take some rope and also a good few of those little crinkly black bags just in case one of them can't wait until we get home.

I don't know how Pear was meant to do his version of this test. Maybe they lent him a roller-skate and a stick to punt himself along with. At the coffee shop the barista – sorry, coffee-making person – will have to shout out *"Small hot chocolate for … Pear."* How are you going to reach it, Pear? Anyway, you only have to find the price; you don't have to actually buy it. Now off you go to the supermarket. No I am not going to give you directions, find it yourself.

My results for the five tasks above were:

1) *Stair Use.* Nailed this one and quickly got back to my old technique. The way I look at it is that stairs are made of horizontal bits and vertical bits – you can't argue with that. Use the horizontal bits to put your feet on and use the vertical bits as an opportunity to lift your body to the next horizontal bit. It's easier than it sounds and it came straight back to me. In fact it is actually easier than escalators where you have to get your walking speed exactly the same as the escalator when getting on and then remember that the up and along bit is actually optional [NOTE TO TOURISTS USING THE TUBE: not optional if on the left side of the escalators]. When getting off you

have to deal with a big group of Spanish teenage girls who stop in a huddle exactly where the escalator stops. You get hurtled right into the middle of the group and before you know it you're at M&M World in Leicester Square. Result: PASS.

2) *Find Shopping Centre.* This was tough without the benefit of a sense of direction. In fact, this was a challenge before I even got properly into the task – I had to find my way out of the ward and not repeatedly into the Assisted Shower room. Once out of the ward I actually didn't know my way to the shopping centre. I hadn't been there before and don't particularly enjoy shopping. In normal life one can ask directions. But not here. We were playing by Smurf Rules and that means no asking and no on-line maps. Result: FAIL.

3) *Film Time.* Got this. Remember, Smurf Rules say: "no using the internet". Some useful information here: the time for the showing of a film I can't remember at a cinema I won't be able to find again, on a day that has passed, is 7.15pm. You never know when that information may come in handy. Anyway my result: PASS.

4) *Price of Milk.* Got this too. There were helpful signs hanging from the ceiling and the one saying "milk" was a useful clue. Unfortunately, being quite a posh supermarket, I had to navigate amongst organic milk, soy milk, rice milk, almond milk, goat's milk … I'm used to straight red, green or blue milk. Got it in the end,

despite there being no sign saying "normal cow milk - you know like you put in tea and that". Answer: 49p. Result: PASS.

5) *Price of Hot Chocolate.* Full marks on this one with my answer:

"Fuck me! A fiver for a small hot chocolate."

Result: PASS.

So, I'm now officially safe to be released back into my natural environment, like one of those rhinos being airlifted in South Africa. In fact I now realise that my skills in pricing milk and milk-based drinks have actually improved. I don't know if there is a particular need out there for people to walk into a cinema and say: "Can you please tell me the time of tonight's showing of [NAME OF FILM] even though I have no intention of seeing it. And by the way, do you have concessions for Smurfs?"

Hair

Everyone knows that cancer sufferers lose their hair. It was therefore expected although still a shock when it happened. I don't really like my hair and so this was bottom of the list of things I had to worry about. If I survive all of this but come out completely bald, I would happily settle for that.

If left to its own devices my hair is frizzy, thick and wiry in a style known amongst north-west London Jews like me as a "Jewfro". That's why I always shave it down to a number two. My surgeon, on the other hand, had amazing hair. It was very long and would be the perfect TV advertising hair for shampoo. He could even toss his hair back in that shampoo advert kind of way. Seeing his hair made me nervously question whether surgeons wear hair-nets? Surely the rules must be stricter for brain surgeons operating than for cooks flipping burgers. My hair had to be shaved at the sides but could be left relatively long at the top. I needed a style compatible with this that was practical, contemporary and gave off an aura of charisma, power and bravado. There was only one way to go: The "Kim Jong Un" complete with nylon sutures all the way round. All I needed was a big red button with "launch" written on it and a fluffy white cat to stroke.

Cinema Trip

I had only been out of hospital a day or so when my University friends came good again. They pitched up and took me and my son Jonah out to see *Godzilla*, followed by chicken and chips. Credit to Carl for following me to the toilets like [NAME OF FAMOUS PERSON REMOVED ON LEGAL ADVICE] to make sure I got there and back without incident or the need for laundry. I found it rather hard to follow the complex plot. All my pieces of skull were loose and being rattled around by the surround sound system. I felt like a jigsaw must feel if being assembled on the back of a moving tractor.

After the film they delivered me to my door and my worried wife. It was like having four carers with me - carers in the well-meaning volunteer kind of way rather than the professional sense.

Benefits

I have never claimed dole or jobseeker's allowance (or whatever it's called these days) in my life. In fact the only "benefit" I have ever received has been child benefit, and that is now a loan, not a nice present from the government. Now this has all changed and I am receiving certain state hand-outs.

Apparently one is entitled to certain benefits as a cancer patient. Things are picking up … until you get into the small print. As an example, I had to surrender my driving licence but was told I may get one of those blue disabled badges. Ah, but I'm much too fit to get a blue badge as I can walk 50 yards. A freedom pass (like a free oyster card)? No, London Borough of Barnet have drowned me in bureaucracy and fail to return calls. There are a few other things that I could potentially get unless I'm fit enough to blink three times in succession without assistance. But here's a benefit I do get: free prescriptions (and believe me, I'm taking a lot of pills at the moment). This is great. A less reputable person could abuse this (and it is tempting) by seeing the doctor and faking the symptoms of other members of the household to get the free medication.

"Yes, doctor, I have suffered for some time with [checks note pad] period pains. I get them every … [I know this, I know this!] four weeks, i.e. at full moon particularly during high tides [now I'm showing off]. I can tell when it's coming as I shout at my husband a lot … Sorry, wife. Now where are these free pills?"

The Leak

In terms of medical scares, I was not home and dry yet. Just when you think things can't get any worse…I experienced a leak.

My recommendation is that you don't read this if you're eating, drinking or about to do either in the foreseeable future. A leak of reddy-yellow stuff out of my nose. That's a good sign, yes? All the bad stuff has been taken out and now we just let the last bit of cancer drip out harmlessly on to the pillow and life gets back to normal.

It's the *lumps* in the leakage that freaked me out. Every single lump to me was potentially a French O-level or similar. This had strange implications for my CV and raises some key questions. Do I now have to start crossing qualifications *off* my CV as I lose them out of my nose? Let's suppose one of the lumps can be identified in the lab as, say, my A grade in economics O-level. If I catch the lump in a pot, do I still have that qualification? If I catch half of it in a pot but the other half goes on the carpet, do I keep the qualification or does it become a B or C grade? It's still my carpet (assuming the leak happens in my house). Maybe the exam board has guidance on this?

Do you feel sick yet?

I was rushed in to see the team at Queen Square and asked "How much has come out?". A cup full? An eggcup full? A spoonful? In which case a teaspoon or a tablespoon? Are they intending to use it as part of a recipe?

I then had the indignity of leaning forward trying to drip nose goo into a pot for them to take "to the lab". Typically, as soon as I was being scrutinised, it all stopped. The embarrassment was putting me off. Every time a drip went in Lu and the nurses congratulated me, like congratulating a two-year-old boy for finally hitting the potty accurately. Of course as soon as we decided to pop out to [NAME OF SHOP REMOVED ON LEGAL ADVICE] for a sandwich, on went the tap. Hooray for [NAME OF SHOP REMOVED ON LEGAL ADVICE] and thanks for all the napkins. Apologies to the other customers, particularly those having the soup.

Basically (and forgive the technical jargon) they needed to establish whether it is nose goo, or brain goo. I asked them how much nose/brain goo they needed. "Ideally quite a few millilitres." Fine – I'm sure I've got loads. Assuming it's brain goo, I'll just leave my poor desiccated brain in the nice dry environment that I'm sure it likes. Shouldn't need too much fluid now the Pear has gone. In fact, now I think about it, the more brain there is, the snugger the fit and therefore the less brain goo required. Also, too much liquid may actually be very distressing for my brain if the knowing-how-to-swim bit of brain was located in the Pear.

So I produced about 1cc from leaning forward and concentrating (excluding the bit on the table at the coffee shop). No sniffing or picking – that's cheating. It must drip out naturally, like fresh morning sap from a maple tree. This "may be enough for the lab". What?! In *CSI* they can work stuff out from a single cell whereas I have to produce half a pot.

In the end it was a leak of brain goo but it sorted itself out. Just as well as I was really not in the mood for a further operation which would have been needed if it did not stop by itself. It would have been a much smaller operation than the Pear-ectomy; just to insert a plastic plug on a nobbly silver chain. For once I got lucky and the leak stopped without a need for a further operation.

Curiosity Day

Now I know which bit of the brain was in the Pear. Basic common sense, or the bit that stops me doing really stupid things for no apparent reason. So what act of genius did pear-brain do? I watched my operation (OK not *my* actual operation but pretty much the same one, on some Korean kid) on-line. It was the most disgusting thing I've seen in my life. Why the hell did I do this? What was I trying to do? Lift my mood or just build an appetite for lunch? In case my life isn't complicated enough I just made it a whole lot harder. Now, to get completely back to normal, not only do I have to stumble across the cure for brain cancer, but I also have to find a time machine so that I can go back to the point in time just before watching the video – i.e., during the pre-video advert bit YouTube make you watch, then tap myself on the shoulder and say *"You're a dick! Watch something else."*

It also raised some questions:

1) What kind of person *wants* to be a brain surgeon? It's an awful job. Couldn't they get a less gory job such as the person who mops up in abattoirs?

2) Who the hell consents to their operation being filmed and then put on-line?

3) And finally, that age-old question: who is cleverer – brain surgeons or rocket scientists? Based upon what they spend their lives looking at (stars and planets versus brain and goo), it must be the rocket scientists.

First Radiotherapy

Radiotherapy follows the operation by about a month. Let me tell you about the set-up for radiotherapy:

They don't want you to move at all, so that the X-rays can be aimed at exactly the right spots. You must be thinking that this will be achieved with a series of clips and straps? But no – in a scenario that's more Ann Summers than NHS, this is achieved by tightly attaching your head to a gurney using a specially modelled, rubber gimp mask. I'm sure the person who invented the procedure was a thoroughly decent, reputable and very intelligent person. However, I suspect I know a tiny bit about his or her preferences in bedroom activities. The whole set-up looks like a cross between the Goldfinger "laser" scene and Fifty Shades of Grey.

So they strapped me down by the gimp mask and hit the lasers. Wait! We haven't agreed our Safe Word yet!

The mask has an open mouth and what can be described as an expression. What's the expression? A terrified scream. As you walk into the radiotherapy suite you see a whole rack of these masks silently screaming at you: "The Treatment – it doesn't really work. And watch out for the man with the axe."

Juicing

So you have a very finite period to live under the shadow of this death sentence. What do you need? Lots of crap advice. In fact there's a whole internet full of it. Apparently one's survival depends upon what you eat and don't eat. No prizes for guessing the kind of things you can't eat: carbohydrates (particularly sugar), alcohol, caffeine and most of all chocolate. So what must you eat? In fact you don't eat, you drink. Fresh juices. Not fruit juices – that's much too pleasant! Vegetable juice, freshly made. Which juicy vegetables must one get up early to press raw each morning? Think of the most succulent vegetable there is; its soft tender flesh literally bursting with sweet, irresistible juice. That's it: broccoli! I borrowed a juicer – a high-power industrial version of the one you may find in a kitchen. In fact broccoli has more juice than you would imagine. You would imagine it to have absolutely none. Whereas the reality is that it has almost none. It's just pound after pound of dry, bitter fibres. That's why it's such a hit with the kids! Anyway, after you've mashed a lump of broccoli into this machine the machine gobs out at you a tiny glassful of green liquid which you then improve with some cucumber and ginger juice. This viscous liquid then tastes a bit like a smoothie made from the blacky-green stuff you might scrape off the grouting in the shower. It really is disgusting. In fact in terms of gastronomic pleasure I rate broccoli juice below chemotherapy tablets (and chemo repeats on you less and makes you feel less sick). There's a reason this juice isn't sold in shops.

Anyway, I have discussed juicing with three different oncologists who each describe it in medical terms as *"complete bollocks"*. One oncologist explained with irrefutable logic:

"If the answer to cancer was broccoli, why would the NHS spend millions and millions on treatments and research?"

I didn't go into the numerous conspiracy theories (check the internet). Something to do with evil drug companies. Either that or a major long-term rift between the NHS and broccoli farmers. Apparently there is information on the internet whose accuracy can be called into question. And yet for months I still juiced those damn broccolis. That means that cynicism did indeed escape from my brain using the Pear as cover.

As time progresses, I am no longer even giving a nod to these diets and recommended foods. I have broccoli just every now and then, and when I do, controversially, I eat the whole thing. No, I do not mean the stalk and that red rubber band the supermarkets inexplicably wrap round it (possibly to increase sales by offering a free piece of stationery). But I eat it, not just squeeze out a teaspoonful of its bitter sap. I also eat chocolate, chocolate ice cream and (look away now if you are of a nervous disposition) drink coffee. To many of my internet advisors, I may as well just throw myself under a train as it is effectively the same thing, although more considerate to commuters.

Infection Day

Part of me thinks that I have now suffered enough for several regular lifetimes and I can indulge in some serious self-pity. I must have used up my entire quota of bad luck for my whole life. Surely nothing worse than stubbing my toe can now happen, otherwise the entire population of the Earth would scream up to Heaven with one deafening voice:

"That's not fair! Leave Adam alone, or else we are all going to dump religion and spend our evenings doing pagan dances around bonfires."

So with all my bad luck used up I can now simply sit back and enjoy my endless lottery wins and OBEs for services to the country in not whining too much about being really, really ill. But it does not work like that. There is an infinite amount of bad luck out there and, for some ridiculous reason I do not pretend to understand, it is not sprinkled evenly amongst the population or, better still, doled out more to really bad people.

This makes other people's good luck a bit infuriating at times. The concept of luck is a relative one compared with the population at large. Therefore, they have good luck because people like me have selflessly (if not willingly) soaked up all the bad luck:

"I would love to hear about the apartment you have hired for the summer in Tuscany, and how little Tarquin is now representing his county in a French Horn knock-out competition."

I am delighted for your good fortune, but luck is all relative. You are lucky because people like me have used up so much of

37

the bad luck. So it should come as no surprise when things like the infection happen despite being in the middle of one of the biggest doses of bad luck ever.

There was another leak – this time from the wound itself and this time pus. OK, it was not brain fluid, but there's not really much that can be seen as reassuring about that. In other words, is a leak of brain-based pus much better than a leak of brain fluid?

We telephoned the hospital – it was a Friday night. We were called in and told to go to A&E. So much for my evening in front of the TV.

We spent the inevitable five hours sitting on uncomfortable, screwed-down steel chairs, waiting and waiting. At one stage there was a fight between a drunk woman and three security personnel. Close thing, but the security team prevailed. My money was on the woman. Eventually I got seen, had another scan and another batch of pills (antibiotics).

I was called back in a couple of days later to see the surgeon who said:

"It looks OK to me. Probably just an infection around the stitches. Worst-case scenario, it is an infection of the skull bone or brain itself, neither of which can be treated with antibiotics."

Can you actually get an infection of the skull or any bone? Isn't it a bit like having an infection of your hair or your shoe? Well, apparently you can get bone infections, as my surgeon told me:

"In the case of brain infection we simply chop out the bit of the brain with the infection. In the case where the skull bone

is infected we chop out a disc of skull for each place where the infection is."

"Just as well my eye infection cleared up then."

"What? Anyway, it is unlikely that we will need to do either of these procedures."

"I have a request if it is my skull that has infections."

"I will of course try to accommodate your request if it doesn't conflict with surgical protocols."

"It's silly really, and I'm sure every single patient with an infected skull requests this."

"Go on. Don't be embarrassed. I'll do what I can."

"I'd like to keep all the skull discs you cut out."

"Er ... OK."

"And I'd like half of them painted red and the other half painted yellow, and leave the very top bit of my head open a tiny bit."

"Er ... Go on."

"And I'd like my head to be turned into a big version of Connect Four."

"Nurse, next patient please and bleep the neuro-psychologist."

"But you're smiling."

"Actually it's trapped wind. Nurse, next patient please and open the window."

Another Psychologist

They do like to keep an eye on me, these NHS bods. I had to go back to the hospital for a consultation with a psychologist. I don't know if it was me or him, but we were not exactly on the same wavelength. My psychologist said to me:

"I understand that you are having unsettling thoughts and feelings at the moment. Do you think you can explain your fears to me?"

"Well, I don't want to die and I'm scared of dying, and of death."

"That's understandable and not uncommon in your situation."

"Isn't everyone sort of against the idea of dying and death, at least in so far as it relates to themselves?"

"Yes, but let's focus on you. Do these thoughts make you feel down, depressed, desperate or in despair? Are there any other similar ways in which you can describe to me the way you feel?"

"Does it have to be with words meaning 'sad' and beginning with a 'd'?"

"Not necessarily."

"[I'M NOT BEING BEATEN BY THIS] I do feel dispirited, disconsolate, despondent, down in the dumps and damned [YES, THAT'S A GOOD ANSWER! 5 EXTRA MARKS AND A BONUS FOR THE DOUBLE: "DOWN IN THE DUMPS". I ALSO KNOW THAT THE THESAURUS ENDED UP IN MY PART OF THE BRAIN AND I NOW KNOW HOW TO NAIL THESE NHS TESTS.]"

"Let's consider your overall state of mental well-being. Have you ever considered suicide?"

"I didn't know that was an option available under the NHS but thanks for trying to help."

"I just wondered if you had experienced any thoughts about a desire to end it all?"

"I appreciate your lateral thinking here to my problem. However, isn't suicide completely contrary to the point. I am scared of death and dying, I'm also undergoing horrendous treatments to (hopefully) delay my death.

So why would I kill myself? What would be the point? That's been taken care of for me."

The psychologist scribbled some stuff down and ticked a box. The box must have been: "No suicide risk", or "Suicide risk but in denial" or most likely "Smart arse".

End of Radiotherapy

It is now a few months since diagnosis and I have had my last radiotherapy session. A huge relief as I hate radiotherapy. However, at the same time, there is a real concern on my part: any cancer cells that have survived to this point are now safe from the zapping and probably stronger too, having managed to survive and be the fittest cells. That's Darwinism for you. However, in proving their ability to survive, they will inevitably end up killing the host (me) as they continue their exponential population explosion. That makes no sense. Maybe the Creationists are right? Anyway, I could get all deep here and create an analogy between the cancerous brain cells within my head and human life on this planet. But I am not going to.

I bought the radiotherapy guys some chocolates and a card because they're very nice. I was allowed to keep my "shell" (a.k.a. gimp mask). I didn't know what to do with it as although I am now really good at radiotherapy, it is not an activity I want to continue with. So what to do with it: lamp shade? Halloween accessory? Or for my own, ahem, bedroom activities? No, too many traumatic memories (relating to the mask I mean, not my bedroom activities). So I chucked it. Despite the cut-backs, the NHS does not recycle these things by finding some patient with the same shaped head as me – i.e. with chiselled classical good looks balanced with a big nose.

More Hair

Now I've finished radiotherapy I am allowed to have my hair cut. With all the bald patches there was only one way to go and shave the lot off exposing quite an impressive bunch of scars. My hair had become quite bushy on the top whilst remaining bald at the sides, like Bert off Sesame Street. On my way to becoming Bert, I was moving down the political food-chain quite dramatically, and in a fortnight had changed from Kim Jong Un to Ed Miliband. But with my new haircut I had now moved up a step to looking like an escaped inmate from Broadmoor. Anyway my barber, Andy, on East Finchley High Road (A & P Barbers, out of the station, turn left and cross the road after 50 yards – free plug for you, Andy) is a top bloke. When I first walked in with my Ed Miliband / Bert-off-Sesame-Street look he thought I'd tried to cut my own hair with clippers but messed it up and I'd come to him to rescue the situation. (I think this is a point that should be noted by Ed M's barber and the puppet creators at the Children's Television Workshop.) Anyway, Andy did a great job and wouldn't accept payment – not even a tip. In fact he gave me a lolly for each of my kids. So I came out in profit and Andy's looking at a place on the A List.

I now have a virtually shaved head and loads of big scars on display. I look really hard. When I walk around the streets of East Finchley, people cross the road to get away from me. When I sit down on a bench, they toss a 20p coin in my direction. This haircut is really working for me.

Despite all Andy's efforts, the final effect of the radiation is a strange one. I am bald on the right side where the radiotherapy went in. I'm also bald on the left in a similar and symmetrical way where the radiotherapy came out. The interaction between the baldness causing radiotherapy going in and the "exit wound" produces a strange effect where the two patterns overlap to create a symmetrical design. It has produced a white shape of baldness on the back of my head against a black background of hair (what's left of it) and the whiteness/baldness clearly resembles, a very particular object: a pair of pants if you must know. White boxer shorts is about as accurate as I can describe it. Of all the things it could have resembled (a unicorn, the peace sign, a silhouette profile of Boris Johnson), I got a pair of pants on the back of my head.

To be fair, not everyone thinks it looks like a pair of pants. My brother, looking at the negative (i.e. the shape of the remaining hair rather than the hole) thought it looked like a phallus and someone else thought it looked like the middle finger of someone "flipping the bird". I think they are just saying this to make me feel better about myself and less self-conscious.

A few weeks later, I popped in to see Andy again for a trim. Not only would he not accept money (not even a tip) but, in total disregard of barber shop etiquette, he also let me jump the queue and pacified all the people in the queue who were sitting there reading the day's tabloids. He then did another smashing job with his electric razor by seamlessly blending my "head pants" into the rest of my bald patches. I now look like an American marine rather than just a weirdo who lost control of the hair clippers.

Magic Beans and Charlatans

I got an article published in *The Times!* In fact it was a much much shorter version of this book but without all the really good bits (yes – there are good bits coming up!). This made me a little bit famous for a while. I also got various unsolicited emails from people who tracked me down through my webpage. This "fan mail" fell into various categories:

1) Genuine appreciation of my ability to present a humorous twist on such an awful situation.

2) Complimenting me on my bravery in writing the article.

3) Trying to make me feel better by telling me stories of various friends and relatives who have got what I have got but managed to go on living well beyond the predicted survival range. So I would be told that somebody's Auntie Val "had what I've got" (how do they know? Have they got my medical records?). Auntie Val smokes three packets of fags a day, drinks half a bottle of gin a day (a whole one on Saturdays) and simply by [INSERT ALTERNATIVE TREATMENT] she has just celebrated her two hundred and thirtieth birthday. What do these so-called doctors know?

4) Emails from crackpots, quacks and magic bean-sellers. Have I tried this remedy/that remedy? They can guarantee it works on all brain tumours and [INSERT VARIOUS ANECDOTAL STORIES ABOUT PEOPLE WITH BRAIN TUMOURS WHO HAVE ACHIEVED IMMORTALITY]. This is accompanied by some pretty heavy doctor-bashing:

"Of course the doctors don't know about this treatment, and if they did, they would never recommend it. You know what doctors are like. So buy these phials of magic water produced in the States at just $200 each. Start off on two a day. The water won't cure you. It empowers your body to cure itself."

What a stupid way of looking at things. If you are given a remedy that causes your body to cure itself, you would be most pedantic to argue that the remedy itself was not the "cure". These people must be a real pain in the arse in their day jobs. Let us suppose they work at a car tyre and exhaust centre:

"We could not fix the exzhaust system and four bald tyres. However, by replacing various parts (including four tyres and the exhaust) we have enabled your Nissan Micra to cure itself. We have also enabled the screen washing to heal itself by topping up the healing blue gooey liquid with our own organic blue gooey liquid which comes all the way from our exclusive supplier in Switzerland and taking away the unhealing dead leaves blocking the healing spray nozzles."

These sales people of alternative remedies speak the same style of rubbish as estate agents, yet we mock the latter but not the former:

"We simply embed these magic electrodes into your brain and your brain simply rejects the cancer cells."

"The solution is these special mushroom spores which have been known since ancient Egyptian times to cure cancers."

Strange, but you would think that Egypt's eradication of cancer would be a little bit better known.

Even my mother has got in on the game. She says that her local supermarket now sell a version of "super broccoli" which is genetically engineered to have all the goodness super concentrated so it becomes a super-effective cancer-busting remedy contained in one inedible side dish. In relation to this one it did not come about from my article. Mum would have been pushing this anyway. I am forty-four years old but really a big kid at heart. As a big kid (or any size kid) I am no longer going to be tricked by my parents into eating vegetables. It is only one step away from being fed the stuff with accompanying steam train noises:

"Quick, before the tunnel closes." (Funny but a nurse said a similar thing before administering a suppository. I just wish that the people responsible for keeping tunnels open had warmer hands.)

5) Various healers. You lie down and let them wave their arms above you in a mysterious and cancer-eradicating way whilst the healer makes her chants. The problem I have is a complete and total inability to take things too seriously or display the appropriate level of reverence. I just can't stop myself. I have to email back saying:

"Please pass my profound thanks on to Sorceress Crystal Willow of Opal the Third. I will come back with some possible times and dates but there may be a little delay as I am jet-lagged - my body is still on Neptune time. Please ask her how much it would cost, in silver presumably, for 10 of her spiritual healing sessions with, say, alternate sessions having a 'happy ending'."

Anyway, it gets me off the mailing lists.

What is amazing is the absolute confidence by which these quacks insist that the cure for cancer is just there, within reach, but these evil and conspiratorial doctors do not want the public to know about it. "You know what doctors are like." Yes I do know what doctors are like. I hang out with enough of them and live with one. I can say with some confidence that, on the whole, they do not have the secret cures to various fatal diseases up their sleeves which they withhold because of some secret pact made with the Devil, or worse, with the big drug companies. The problem with doctors is that when they get together at, say, a dinner party they can get very boring - particularly when they tell a tale of one of their great medical successes or failures using only acronyms. It can be like a conversation with someone

49

who makes all their points by flinging Scrabble letters at you. In fact doctors in small numbers can be great fun. Way, way back I remember an A & E junior doctor absolutely enrapturing a dinner party by recounting the story of a man who came in to Accident & Emergency with a 2-litre (yes, I said TWO LITRE) bottle of cola shoved up his backside. By the time we had asked all the questions, this little fable had kept us entertained for the entire evening. I mean what terrible luck to slip off the chair like that whilst wearing a loose dressing gown (and nothing else) before having a chance to clear up the soft drinks. And of all the places the bottle could have made impact with the body, what are the chances of contact happening between the top of the bottle and "that bit", and the angle being exactly "right". This guy sounds even less lucky than me. I will allow him to use my expression "Fuck my luck" although he may wish to adapt it to remove any perceived sexual overtones. Hopefully he has got it out by now (in not too painful a manner) and can leave the expression to those of us who really need it. I wonder if they got Norris McWhirter round for the removal procedure to observe and verify the World's Greatest Sigh of Relief. This doctor, she informed us, had told the story a number of times. Apparently the question most commonly asked is: Was it full of cola and if so, what happened to the drink? Strange how the human mind can latch on to some trivial detail. Like having a brain tumour and getting obsessed by the fruit it most resembles in size and shape. All I can say is that you must be pretty desperate for a glass of pop to even consider drinking it after that, particularly as you would have to wait some time for it to chill properly from a cosy 37 degrees (and who would allow that thing in their fridge?).

Going back to my categories of emails. Number 2. I really don't see myself as "brave". It is not that I am a self-hater or something like that. I just don't think that writing stuff about how crap (and short!) life has turned out is particularly brave. Let's be clear about this – I am writing this book in the hope of raising money for my wife and family when I snuff it. I would also like to be on popular panel shows and be really famous and loved by everyone. That is not brave. An example of being brave is running into a burning building to rescue a baby from the top floor. Bravery has two elements:

1) Doing an act voluntarily that puts yourself in danger, and
2) Doing so for a purely selfless reason.

I satisfy neither of these criteria.

Let me dwell a little further on the alternative remedy sales people / quacks / charlatans. Here is the problem: All potential buyers (myself included) are completely desperate. If you do not have cancer you can approach subjects like this with an element of sensible objectivity and rational cynicism. But us cancer-sufferers are plagued by the "What ifs" that go round and round our head at night. When death is just round the corner, wasting five grand is not a massive deal in the scheme of things. However, turning away a remedy that lets me cure myself is a tragedy. What if, what if, what if. It drives me mad to the point where I buy and juice broccoli. I send details of all of these potential "cures" to my brother-in-law, Alan, who is a professor of oncology. Alan then lets me have the readings on his "Bollocks-o-meter" (named by truth levels of what it detects, and not where it is kept) which is always off the scale. Desperate people do stupid things and I don't want people to visit my grave thinking

"What a twat. If only he had taken that extract of magic unicorn tears he would be up here now with the living."

So desperate and dying people do stupid things with their money. The charlatans know this. Luckily I have people to give me a sharp kick up the backside when I am about to get the cheque book out. But I have a plan which should please both the cancer sufferers and the magic bean-sellers. It may not please the doctors but you know what those doctors are like! The quacks are absolutely confident that they can cure me with their rare and expensive magic beans. They have so many stories of people they have cured – in fact they must be well on their way to a sainthood. I am a profound cynic with one of these horrible incurable diseases told at length by doctors that none of these remedies work and the evidence does not stack up or even exist. Accordingly, I need at least three people in white coats to endorse anything I am taking.

Now what if these charlatans (and I use this term in the affectionate sense) change their business terms in the following way? Then I'd sign up to everything going. I would pay £5,000 for these magic beans. My scheme is that payment should only be made on the tenth anniversary of the date of purchase and only be paid strictly conditionally upon the patient being alive on this payment date. Everyone's a winner! I would happily spend £5,000 or even £10,000 on a cure provided it really is a cure. The charlatans get their money and huge sales, albeit on very generous credit terms. Waiting ten years for the money is a small price to pay as the effective "interest" can simply be rolled into a higher purchase price. If they are worried about getting the money out of the patient they needn't be:

1) I would be so thrilled to live that I would pay it happily and may even send a bottle of wine or a cake too, and I am sure that others would feel like this.

2) The money could be held in a form of escrow a bit like a tenant's deposit scheme. The charlatans that do not sign up to this arrangement are clearly just on the make and, difficult as it may be to believe, may not have our best interests at heart.

London Borough of Barnet

You might think that when you are living with a terrible disease that could mean you are dead way before your time, it is only the important things in life that matter and the trivialities of everyday life wash over you. Don't believe a word of it. Let me tell you about my experiences with my council, London Borough of Barnet (or "LBB" as it is affectionately known). Now I am officially disabled I have plenty of dealings with them, unfortunately.

The bin men came this morning. Usual enough for a Thursday morning. However, this time they had wedged the refuse bin (black bin) and the recycling bin (blue bin) into the narrow path up to the house, with the handles facing the outside (i.e. road side). My whole family had been imprisoned by the bin men. Technically I am disabled because of my illness and LBB know this. I have to admit that I was not totally trapped and could make it out of my property (by jumping over the fence to next door), and I did not have to consider seriously for long the prospect of having to call the Coastguard or Mountain Rescue. But still. When you contact a large company you get:

"Thank you for contacting us" or

"Your call is important to us" or

"We wish all our customers a happy Christmas/Easter/ Holiday Season/Yom Kippur" etc.

So what do I love about LBB? It has this this rare and raw honesty that means the council and its staff do not even pretend to give a shit. Once you have finally managed to speak with a human after penetrating the LBB switchboard their attitude is crystal clear:

"Yes, I have now listened to your whining. Tell me your phone number. I'm not going to write it down. However, if, tomorrow, I can still remember the number, your name and what the hell you were moaning on about, I will pass this on to a minion a lot further down the food chain than me who could quite possibly ring you back and make you tell the story all over again before doing nothing about it. This should occur within the next seventy-two working days. If this issue concerns your physical or mental health please complete form IHBE1014 online, print it out and deliver it in triplicate to office 6127 at the Town Hall. Our team of dedicated caseworkers will process this form and, if your application is successful, we will send to you, free of charge, our booklet: 'Help! I'm Becoming Enfeebled, And The Council Is Getting Right On My Tits'. This booklet is also available in large print, braille and as an audio leaflet."

Shortly after my diagnosis Lu applied for a Freedom Pass for me (basically, a bit like a free Oyster Card for the disabled, giving me access to the whole of London's public transport network). Lu spent an hour or so filling in a complicated online application form, complete with personal and medical details, then hit the "submit" button and waited. Nothing. Not for an hour; in fact not for a month. She phoned up a few times to get to the bottom of it. Apparently the online form does not work and all data put into it just falls into an electronic black hole. A huge melting pot of individuals' sensitive personal data and details of their unfortunate circumstances. Every now and then the black hole gets emptied by the bin men who will casually discard the bins trapping in the remaining data and preventing it leaving home. If they cannot fix this part of the website, why do they not flash up a message saying:

"This electronic form does not work" or

"You're about to needlessly lose two hours of your life" or

"To be filling in this form you will, no doubt, be quite seriously disabled or ill and in need of this vital assistance, but: .... screw you!"

Unfortunately, they cannot fix the e-form nor stick up a message saying it's broken. It must be fiendishly complicated and difficult to do this. They must simply be waiting for an available Professor at MIT to be able to fly over and re-engineer the website to put this message up.

So completing an LBB online form is just shoving some data in its general direction in the misplaced hope that the information will be received, collated, processed and acted upon. It's the electronic equivalent of throwing a paper form in the general direction of the Town Hall hoping that this will get you some kind of specific and relevant assistance.

A Further Psychologist

I saw another psychologist a few weeks after the first one to see if I was improving at all. The new psychologist started by asking:

"How are you? Can you explain to me what you are feeling?"

"I don't want to die but I'm dying. I am scared of death and yet this is happening pretty soon. I don't think I have left sufficient money for my family to live comfortably after my death so I have taken the desperate step of writing a book, when I have no relevant experience, so that my family is going to be able to live off the royalties. The little life I have left is stressful, packed with unpleasant medical treatments and bad statistics and possibly not worth living. How are you?"

"Fine, thanks. You are entitled to have those feelings. They are a natural reaction to what you are going through."

"I was entitled to scream and shout 'X%&+@@$$*£*!!!' when I dropped that hammer on my toe the other day, but it didn't actually help."

"Is there anything you think I can do that may help your situation?"

"You could buy my book."

She was a very nice lady but looked quite shocked and beaten by the end. Perhaps not up to debating with someone as difficult as me.

I think I need a new psychologist – I've broken this one. For one thing she did not even think of asking a very obvious question:

"Do you have any superpowers that may have been affected by the operation and subsequent treatments?"

Exercise

I am trying to keep myself in reasonable shape despite the continuous tiredness from my treatment, nausea and apathy. I try to do some weights and fairly regularly go running. Unfortunately, last time I went running I got lost in Highgate Woods. For those of you unfamiliar with North London, Highgate Woods is not an endless rolling Scandinavian-type forest, reaching the horizon in all directions. It's a patch of trees and a playground, completely fenced off at the perimeter and with a single path doing a circular lap. Therefore one should never be able to get lost: you just go in any direction in a roughly straight line until you hit the fence and then you follow the fence round to the correct exit. All I need is the ability to distinguish gate from fence (I can do that! Gates are more permeable) and the ability to read "East Finchley, this way" (I can do that too. Pear didn't get the reading bit of my brain or at least not all of it).

I bet the Pear is sniggering away to himself right now from wherever he is; in some lab somewhere, with a smug little smile on his smug little temporal-lobey face, from up on the shelf, floating in his jar of vinegar, knowing that he ended up with the sense of direction, spatial awareness and quite a lot of the logic functions. Well screw you, Pear! You may have ended up with those things, but I ended up with the blood supply! And the CD collection. Oh, and the eyes, so you're not reading this unless that nice neuro psychologist is reading it to you in his lunch hour. And has found you some ears.

For the last fifteen years or so I have been regularly going to the gym. I find the cardio machines very boring but love the therapy of pounding the weights. My first gym was quite a rough place in the heart of Kilburn. No women wearing make-up and speaking on mobile phones in there. You know the type of ladies I am talking about: posh leotards and leggings and all their clothes looking like they were put on in reverse order with leotard underneath and underwear-type clothing of a totally different colour on the top. In fact I was the only one going to that gym who was not a bouncer or cage fighter. Loads of huge, muscly, sweaty blokes who looked upon me as a kind of Charles Hawtrey character. I would spend an hour or so doing a bit of everything in terms of muscles. The other gym goers may, for example, spend a straight two hours lifting unfeasibly huge weights, the equivalent of a small car, just using their outer calf muscles. I will let you in on a little secret. Contrary to what non-gym goers may think, weight lifting is not macho at all but really quite camp. This was brought home to me once when watching someone train with their gym buddy. The bloke working out was in a semi-squat position (you know, like when you cannot decide whether or not to have a bowel movement), half crouching down and sticking his backside out backwards towards his buddy. The bar with the weights was at knee-level and the exercise was to pull the bar into the bottom of his stomach or the top of his groin. Meanwhile the gym buddy (with loads of muscles bulging out from one of those wife-beater vests) would stand right behind him with a hand on each of the guy's hips shouting:

"Pull in harder. Yes!! That's a good length."
Before mincing round to the front and saying:
"OK, let's hit the showers."

This gym closed down which made me very sad and I had to move on to posh gyms which I liked less. My first "posh gym" was in a hotel and was called "Living Well". I can remember the name easily as it sounds like a mixture of "Living Will" and "Living Hell". It was not the gym for me. I like my gyms to smell of sweat and to echo with the sound of Neanderthal grunting.

I suspended my gym membership as soon as I got ill as inevitably, when the time came, I would choose a nap over working out, and so my membership was no longer good value. Recently, though, I have gone back to my personal trainer for a few sessions a month, just to keep things ticking along. My PT, Mervin, is superb at his job and an excellent bloke. In an all too familiar scenario he wanted to refuse payment from me. We have now compromised and he will work for "mates' rates" on the strict condition (his condition, not mine) that I have at least one free "sesh".

Merv, you are on the A List. I slightly overdid it the first time. I woke up the day after the session and every single part of me ached depending upon what movement I was undertaking, and when I sneezed, every muscle in my body hurt simultaneously. I suppose this was to be expected after a few months off.

New Friends

Using internet forums, Lu has made a new friend, Mandy, wife of Mike the latter having a GBM tumour like me. [NAMES CHANGED FOR ANONYMITY – EXCEPT LU IS LU] It's nice that Lu can find someone with similar fears, going through the same trauma as her and, in this way, the two wives can support each other. I am in awe of Mike because he had his tumour on the left side. Apparently the lobes of the brain on the left side are better and more important than the equivalent ones on the right, or so the neurologists say. (Hang on. Isn't that all a bit "lobist" or something?) Speech is on the left side, for example. I am in even more in awe of Mike because he had to have his operation whilst being kept awake and talking to them.

I wonder what they chatted about? Is it like the conversation with your barber, or the type of chat you have with your dentist whilst he is delving around in your mouth. *"Going anywhere nice this summer?"* And then he shows you the hole with that little hand-held mirror pointed at the back of your head whilst you nod approvingly.

Lu and Mandy are trying to make arrangements for the four of us all to get together, but so far we have not met. I don't want to sound like a miserable, antisocial and heartless git but, whilst I have no reason to think that we won't get on, there is no particular reason I can see why Mike and I should get on any better than, say, me and some completely random person picked off the street. Whilst friends normally share the same interests or outlook on life, I don't think this quite counts in our situation. Imagine me hosting a party to which my new friends

Mike and Mandy are invited. I might say to a guest:

"Let me introduce you to my good friend, Mike. Funny story how we met. Anyway, we get on so well because we are both dying of exactly the same disease. Ain't that right, Micky?"

This also reminds me of a friend I used to mock endlessly because he joined a club for people who owned a certain type of flashy sports car he had bought – an MG something or other (I was not interested enough to remember it). That was the thing the members of this club all had in common: really small dicks. I told him I had joined a club for people who own the same toaster as me, a Home Uni-Slot Toaster "Life Extra" (or "Hustlers" as we used to acronym ourselves). Us Hustlers like the fact that you can use the toaster to heat up and brown (or "toast", to use the technical jargon) bread types as varied in shape, dough-type, originating culture *and* thickness as a bagel and a chapatti. Jumping from East Coast USA to Southern Asia during the course of the same meal. And there's a little tray at the bottom with which you can neatly slide out all those troublesome toast crumbs. No turning the toaster upside down and banging it over the sink for me and the other Hustlers. We all understand that in each other and it bonds us.

Anyway, back to my non-existent party. The wives can just make out the odd sentence or two of the conversation between Mike and me. In fact I have a really loud voice (as I'm told by the people who share an office with me or have an office in the next pod or town) and Mike is fairly quiet (he is my "imaginary" friend so I get to pick his characteristics) and so they'd probably only hear snippets from my half of my conversation with Mike. Here is what it must sound like:

"…… and when she pulled it out, my ears went pop."

"…… and she said to me: 'I am just saying that we don't normally test for MRSA there'."

"Diarrhoea, constipation, diarrhoea, constipation; constantly alternating. My life is a roller-coaster in every sense at the moment."

"So the instructions on the box of suppositories say: 'Take one after each bowel movement; no more than four in a day.' Well, which is it?"

"Yes, the little tray just slides out and you can tip those crumbs straight into your composting box."

Time with My Daughter

I do this very cute thing with my daughter, Thea, who is five years old. I often say to her:

"Thea, who's your favourite Daddy?"

To which she replies:

"You, Daddy. You are my favourite Daddy."

Then she sometimes gives me a big hug. She is very intelligent, of course, and sometimes qualifies this with:

"But you are my only Daddy."

This qualification by Thea undermines the beauty of the situation a little, whilst at the same time is a bit reassuring (bearing in mind my long hours and the many evenings I am out).

Anyone watching this exchange goes all unnecessarily gooey with that kind of sympathetic sad look where the mouth goes into a small "o", the eyes narrow as if about to cry, the head cocks about 30 degrees to one side or the other and the hands do that motion where they are cupped together and it looks like they are driving a small imaginary dagger into the person's own heart – only a stabbing to the heart could properly represent the true emotional impact that this interplay between Thea and me demonstrates.

Anyway, occasionally I make one tiny adjustment to this question:

"Thea, who's your favourite Daddy."

Just one subtle change, and there are no looks of adoration from onlookers or, indeed, Thea. One tiny refinement to a single word and the reactions change dramatically:

"So Thea, who's your favourite parent?"

Onlookers tut, roll their eyes and go all weird and critical. The answer is *"me"* by the way, seeing as I ask the question just before dishing out chocolate.

Fertility

I am told by the medics that my fertility will be dramatically reduced by the chemotherapy. Before starting treatment, the doctor asked us if we were planning on having more children. Sounds like a sensible question – yes? However, Lu and I both hurt ourselves falling off our respective chairs laughing. The conversation ended when I answered the doctor:

"Only if you agree to do some pretty regular babysitting."

If Lu gets pregnant in the next few months I can boast:

"So who's the Daddy?!"

and hope that it is a rhetorical question posed as a kind of boast of manhood rather than a genuine enquiry regarding parentage.

Trials

Standard NHS treatments do not cure brain tumours like mine but simply buy time. Therefore people in my position look towards the trials partly out of desperation. These are basically experiments and we are scurrying around to see where the most promising place is to take on my role as a lab rat.

Opportunities for trials are around. However, if they are not in the UK, it becomes very expensive indeed. It seems odd that I have to pay to be involved in the experiments. Do the lab rabbits make payment to cosmetic companies to have shampoo dripped into their eyes?

One trial that looks exciting is based on use of cannabis derivatives. I imagine a big group of us patients sprawled out on beanbags in the ward passing round a giant joint. This would be followed by a balloon-debate style argument as to which one of us must get up and go to the 24-hour garage to get the crisps and bars of chocolate. In fact it is not like that at all. Apparently when asked how you would like to take the cannabis the answer is not: joint, bong, hash brownies or pipe. The correct answer is:

"I'd like the THC distilled out of the cannabis and then injected directly into my brain whilst my skull is opened up."

Maybe this is the ultimate way to take it although I see obstacles to this taking off with recreational users.

Many of the promising trials look to be in America, which is also the most expensive place to be treated. Literally hundreds of thousands of dollars per trial. This is a very difficult kind of amount. If the treatment costs, say, five million dollars, there would be a final, definite and clear *"No"*. It is impossible. If everything was laid on for free except, say, the peanuts for the flight over, then that would be pretty clear too: "Yes – go for it".

We are in the difficult middle ground where the money could just about be raised in theory (for example, by selling the house or each of us selling a kidney or two). However, that would leave the family impoverished and possibly living in the shed with our family's dialysis machine (which we would need, having sold our kidneys). This is not a scenario I am prepared to leave as my legacy should the trial be unsuccessful.

This is the kind of question that rattles around the remnants of my brain at three o'clock in the morning:

"How much should we, as a family, spend on my treatment, and therefore how much debt should the household take on, in the hope that it will cure me or at least pay for itself in terms of extending my ability to work?"

It is very difficult to come up with a figure. However, after agonising over it and deciding what can be shaken out of my extended family, the conclusion is a number with six digits. For the smart arses out there: six digits to the left of the decimal point, and the currency is sterling. When our true value is condensed down to a single figure signifying our entire financial "worth", life (or what's left of it) does get very depressing. It reminds me of when I handed our two pet goldfish over to my parents to look after whilst we went on holiday. I reminded my parents that the fish were well loved and of great sentimental value to all of us, especially my son, Sacha. In the event of an untimely death in the tank, nothing could ever replace Goldie or Lawrence in our hearts (my children chose the name "Goldie" and I was responsible for the name "Lawrence". What? It's a perfectly good name for a goldfish!) That said, we need to be sensible, practical and, above all, commercial about these arrangements. We must not forget that my parents are doing us a favour here. Therefore, in the event that either Goldie or Lawrence kicks the bucket whilst we are on holiday, I would be looking to my parents for reimbursement of the entire 95 pence per fish only, being the replacement price in our local pet shop. This has now come back to bite me, particularly as I realise how few fish I am equivalent to. If we were debating how much we would spend on experimental and potentially life-saving treatment for either of the fish I think that 95 pence would form a sensible cap for the maximum amount we would spend. Now I think about it, this means that, in terms of money to be spent on life-saving treatment measured in pounds sterling per gram of body mass, the fish are more valuable than me. And Lawrence was won at a fair! Anyway, I am not speaking to the fish at the moment.

Brighton Pier

We went to Brighton to see my in-laws. We took a friend of my middle son, Sacha. Because of my illness I have a very strong desire to avoid places which are noisy, busy or chaotic. So where did we visit? That's it: the arcade at the end of Brighton Pier. Sacha and his friend are both addicted to, and rather good at, the penny falls. In fact, as a moderately well-off family we play the 2p falls – we are middle-class after all, yet we're also not quite lavish enough to fit in with the posh brigade who play the 10p falls – those flash gits. Feeding in silver coin after silver coin is just too rich and showy for us. Yet we look down on the cheapskates playing with penny coins. My view is that everyone in society should simply know their place, and this is ours.

I have always worked on the principle that, with gambling, on average you lose. That cannot be wrong as otherwise the various bookmakers and fruit machine operators would be charitable organisations or go out of business. Yet our boys seemed to be winning 2p coins at exactly the same rate that they were feeding them into the machines. They were breaking the "Number One Rule" in the Gambling Rule Book: punters lose! (at least on average they do). I don't actually know any other rules in the Gambling Rule Book other than the one about pens and pencils provided being absolutely tiny.

I wanted to get away from the bleepy noises, flashing lights and tattoos, as quickly as possible. It was like some Kafkaesque nightmare where it went on and on. If the boys were at least winning then my nightmare would eventually end when the machines all emptied; but I was in my own hellish world of gambling equilibrium. What next? Normal sized pens and pencils? What is it with my luck at the moment? First I develop a very rare type of brain tumour. If that's not enough, a couple of months later I get trapped in a wrinkle in the time space-time continuum, placing me in my everlasting cycle of noisy, gambling hell.

At last the kids' two pence coins ran out. I could have kissed those unpleasant-looking people in their nylon uniforms with their impossible-to-win machines from hell.

At this arcade, not only did you win coins but the various machines also spat out these paper tokens that look like raffle tickets. The idea is that you save them up and, depending upon the number of tokens, redeem them for certain prizes. Thus completing the cycle of:

1) a useful one pound coin, to

2) a pot of fifty 2p coins together with various bits of tissues, people's viruses and other unpleasantness, to

3) different soiled coinage; then to

4) hundreds of toilet paper quality pieces of pink paper which in turn get converted into

5) some plastic junk manufactured in Asia at, no doubt, great cost to the environment.

Anyway we won hundreds of those damn tokens. Which you then take to the special desk and check against the "price chart" to see which toy or other reward your child can "afford" with this new ticket currency, and get frustrated with before it breaks the following day. I don't want to get all political here but why doesn't Brighton Pier form a currency union with the rest of the UK and use "money". Our boys had enough tokens (about 500) to redeem two plastic guns that fire foam-covered plastic bullets. This way the family could spend the rest of the relaxing weekend as if trapped in the cross-fire between two rival south London gangs. They could have instead redeemed them for a large teddy bear which doesn't make a noise nor constantly pelt you with bullets. If we had acquired 500,000 tokens I could redeem them for participation in an American brain tumour trial (possibly) but alas – plastic guns it was.

The Punt Trip

Hanging out with my university friends can be a traumatic experience but it is always fun. From the moment of the first handshake up to final manly goodbye hugs, it is one big circus of piss-taking and abuse. Received from all directions and dished out to all. I am not talking clever wit – Oscar Wilde we ain't. It's puerile and toilet-based humour of the lowest order. To give you an idea of the kind of level of humour (in case you imagined for a moment, there was clever word play in action or playfully contradictory literary references) the punchlines end up falling into one of the following categories:

1) Something toilet-related.

2) Some description of a body part or something that comes out (or is coming out) of one of our bodies.

3) "Your Mum."

Every year we celebrate our inability to come up with a new category of humour by getting together in Cambridge for our annual Punt Trip to Grantchester. We have done this now for twenty-five years on the trot. I have only missed one trip and that was because I was living in Lesotho at the time. In the year immediately following graduation, I was a teacher at a very remote mountain school in this tiny mountain kingdom. I taught maths and science to secondary school students in a school that was more than six hours' journey from the nearest telephone. A fantastic and life-enhancing year, only marred by the absence of a punt trip.

The Punt Trip is an all-male occasion. It is not that we are sexist or anything (well I'm not), but women have this unwanted civilising effect on us and so to truly let the caveman in us off the leash, no women are allowed. It is not just this civilising effect that excludes our female friends. To attend a Punt Trip there is a practical requirement that each participant can urinate off a moving punt (without getting their feet wet) – punts do not tend to have on board facilities. And don't rely upon any assistance from the other passengers, who will inevitably rock the punt in a jerky fashion at the critical moment.

We fill the punt to the brim with cider, wine, beers and various other alcoholic drinks as well as sandwiches, crisps, biscuits, chocolates, cakes and sweets. It looks as if we cannot decide whether to participate in a tramps' away day or a five-year-old's birthday tea party. Choosing the delights for our al fresco lunch is one of the highlights of the trip and my M&S trolley dash marks the beginning of this auspicious day.

So why do I subject myself to, and participate in, such crude and childish playground banter? Why do I subject my fragile body and vulnerable state of mind to twenty-four hours of non-stop abuse? I have various theories to assist here:

a) Every bloke is, at heart, a caveman. The caveman must be allowed out every now and then to get him out of our systems. This way we can get all (OK, most) of our bad behaviour out in a controlled way, in an isolated environment and not in front of a client, senior colleague, frail relative or in a place of worship.

b) It's fun; really fun. I come back rejuvenated mentally (not physically, of course). At the end of the Punt Trip my body is a groaning mess and a further reminder of my own mortality and the effects of the ageing process.

c) It takes us back in time to an era when everything was less stressful and nothing needed to be serious. None of us used words like "commitment", "responsibility" or "sanitary".

d) None of the Boys do that wincey/pained/empathetic look. That is great because I don't have to find the right expression in return. I never know whether to respond with the "hurt puppy" look or the "strong and stoical" look as if we were simply debating ways for me to get over an unpleasant remark.

e) Most importantly, the Punt Trip is an opportunity to be submerged in the past for a day. The care-free, uncomplicated, unstressful and un-cancery past.

However, I have noticed with deep sadness that we are starting to get more and more civilised on these trips (despite the absence of women). Depressingly so as we have "grown up" and in some cases had children. In our undergraduate days a typical snippet of conversation might be:

"Oi Kim, why are you tipping that cider into the river when you've only drunk seven bottles. And why did you put that chicken leg in Gary's pocket? I was still chewing on the bone – give it back." [INSERT PREDICTABLE PUNCHLINE FROM CATEGORY 2) [BODY PARTS] AND/OR 3) INCLUDING THE PHRASE "YOUR MUM".]

Now it is more likely to be:

"Has anybody seen the wet-wipes? Gary sensibly brought some anti-bacterial hand gel but I find that so terribly drying to the skin and it may reduce the effectiveness of the sun cream." Or *"I cannot believe we only brought one type of mustard this year. It wouldn't hurt anyone to have packed a small jar of Dijon and an extra mustard spoon. Don't blame me! – I was responsible for condiments last year."*

I wonder if there is still a single reader who still believes that we behave as one would imagine Cambridge undergraduates or graduates stereotypically behave at a reunion. To assist you in calibrating our combined level of intellect on a punt trip, it took us twenty-four years to realise that it was far cheaper to hire the punt for a day at the day rate than to pay by the hour. This is particularly the case for groups like ours with some quite skilled punters to get us there in well under an hour but where we fall asleep at Grantchester meadows, play cricket for a couple hours and get too drunk to navigate the way back without going down every last tributary.

The level of conversation is really brought home when I get back to Lu and I am debriefed:

"So how was Kim and how is his job going?"

"I don't know, we didn't talk about that."

"Gary? Carl?"

"Didn't talk about their jobs, health or lives either. We were busy talking about other stuff."

"You were with them for twenty-four hours, what did you talk about? Don't you take an interest in each other's lives?"

"Yes, of course we do. Kim is still a teacher I think. Can't remember where but probably at a school. Nothing he said suggested this has changed."

"What about Carl?"

"He still has that job somewhere doing that thing with computers,......but he may have left." [Carl does not have children and consequently has no need for money.]

"Gary?"

"His bowels are still performing sub-optimally."

"Oh, is that what he said?"

"No, it was just kind of obvious."

The best thing of all about the Punt Trip is that for twenty-four hours, we just talk rubbish. Not a word of sense or the passing on of any information. Nobody uses the word 'feeling' other than in a sexual context or a 'feeling that we need to stop in a field urgently'.

It was a classic Punt Trip this year and we relived some of the best moments of past trips. For example there was the year Kim admitted that only one of the three of us had been invited to his wedding (not me, grr). The reason being (according to Kim) that the venue was too small for everyone and, regrettably, we did not make the cut. According to me, he had simply got the wrong venue and got his list of potential guests in the wrong order and applied the wrong criteria, the correct criteria being how much of a laugh we each are. On this basis I clearly beat parents of the bride and many of the elderly relatives on Kim's side. Yet they were invited, not me!

This year was a bit different in that everyone was being nice to me. The normal insults were regularly punctuated by

"Oi, are you all right, Ad?" and

"Ad, shouldn't you get out of the sun?"

Gary, being a senior teacher, is probably the most responsible and so Lu gave him the task of administering my pills, a job which he took very seriously. It was also universally agreed that I would not get pushed into the river and therefore would avoid a dose of the famous 'Cam Fever' (a really quite unpleasant water - borne bacteria and not a funky seventies disco hit). Gary also picked me up at the beginning of the day and dropped me all the way home the next, delivering this important little package back to Lu in a state where I was functioning virtually normally.

Prognosis and Maths

It has been six months since the discovery of the Pear. So what is my prognosis? Apparently 5 per cent of people with my diagnosis become 'long-term survivors'. I don't know the definition of 'long-term' in this context but presumably it is not measured from the mayfly perspective.

The median survival is eighteen months after diagnosis. In other words (for the non-mathematicians) if you hypothetically line up all the people who have had this cancer in the fairly recent past, in strict order with the longest duration survivors at one end and the shortest at the other (they may need propping up somehow), the median is the survival length of the middle person. It is a form of 'average'. Yes, I know – what if there are an even number of people? I won't go into the detail here, but the statisticians can cope with that. There are some things in my favour though, which improve my chances:

1) I'm classified for these purposes as 'young' (nice to hear this as a 44-year-old).

2) I'm also classified as 'fit' – also nice to hear.

3) My surgeon did a blindingly good job of chopping out the bastard Pear.

Whilst I am in my bedroom howling at my terrible luck, I try to put a positive spin on this. Importantly it does not mean (or necessarily mean) I'm going to live eighteen months from diagnosis. The lower end of the survival curve will hopefully be soaked up by the old and unfit, or people who had a surgeon on an off day. I say "hopefully" not in the sense of wanting anything bad to happen to my brain-tumoured friends, but it is pear eat pear out there and we have all got to fight for the top spots in the statistical curve. Once I have 'reserved' my top spot and this is set in stone, I want everyone lined up to live as long as possible, just not at my expense. Of course us brain-tumour sufferers are all statistically independent and we are not actually in competition with each other. However, if I manage to take one of the top spots I will have this nagging guilt that, by doing so, I have selfishly bumped someone down into the "below eighteen months" half. Despite this last point being complete rubbish in terms of logic, this is how my grieving brain (or what's left of it) deals with the maths and the guilt. More telling than all this is the fact that my wife (an oncologist, I remind you) is in tears:

1) every night and
2) every time we discuss an event more than a year or so into the future.

I think that says it all.

Alan

I have discussed all of this at length with Lu's brother, Alan. Alan is also an oncologist and a professor at the cutting edge of the research into finding cures for cancer. I am therefore in the interesting position where my brother-in-law's job is to put my wife (being his sister) out of work. Al has been a top guy over the last few months (and is generally). He fields all the calls from my concerned relatives when they bombard him with questions about statistics and outcomes, and he brings a good element of sanity into Lu's and my crazy and chaotic lives.

Naturally I have been agonising over why I have been struck down by this illness. Mobile phone usage? Radio masts placed in residential areas? Too many burgers of questionable origin when I was a student? Being hit in the head by a low flying bat (the animal, not the object) several times during my lifetime? (To be clear, I suspect it was a different bat on each occasion rather than one single bat with a vendetta against me.) Apparently it is none of these. There is no environmental reason for a brain tumour. In fact it is not genetic either, so I can't even blame my parents. I am told that for no reason anyone has established, some of my brain cells have simply gone haywire and multiplied like crazy. It is completely random who gets it. A bit like being struck by lightning or having a piano dropped on you from a tall building during a bizarre and incompetent moment of furniture moving.

This puts a different spin on things. I have nobody to curse, not even myself. My motto has become *"Fuck my luck!"*, which I scream out of the window at night every so often and which

I have asked to be engraved on my tombstone as my parting words to this universe.

This also causes the unfortunate turn of events to have a particular philosophy. What has happened really is just fate, which is strangely comforting. It is written in the stars and can never be changed that Adam Blain will only celebrate a single birthday where his age begins with a number five (my fifth birthday, in case you haven't worked it out).

Alan understands all of this. He, tragically, was randomly struck down by a terribly debilitating stroke some years back which affects his movement and mobility considerably. However, he does not scream *"Fuck my luck!"* This is partly because he is a positive and accepting person, and partly because this is my expression and he is not allowed to use it.

Anyway, I could not have made it this far without Alan.

Distribution of Possessions

Being the morbid person I am, I have given some thought as to how my possessions should be divvied up on my death. Most of it to my wife Lu obviously, but there may be some stuff for friends and family. Of course Lu gets anything valuable, sentimental or useful. I want to avoid any conversations such as Lu saying to me:

"I haven't seen your wedding ring for a while. Also, I have just cooked some broccoli as you requested. You haven't seen the colander have you?"

"Yes, a friend always had her eye on the colander and I said it comes with a wedding ring as a promotional gift."

In fact the wedding ring is a bad example. I'm not giving it to anyone other than Lu. She definitely wants to keep it and, to be perfectly honest here, she has a better moral claim to it than many of my past and present friends and colleagues.

My fingers are not elegant piano-player's fingers. They are pudgy and unsightly. The type of fingers you would imagine Homer Simpson to have but, perhaps, a bit less yellow. The ring is going to be much too big for Lu's delicate digits. However, she has already thought of this and come up with a solution: she is going to wear my wedding ring around her neck. Since my Pear-removal op I do question my own logic from time to time, particularly when it is at odds with the logic of someone else who I know is clever (Lu, for example). Lu is quite petite and elegant. However, she does not really have the fine features of the Kayan Lahwi tribeswomen. There is simply no way the ring will fit around her neck without certain strangulation. Furthermore, despite being nearly perfectly proportioned, how will she get it over her head in the first place?

I don't always understand the female sequence of logic so I checked the position with a different female brain (a friend) to see which one of us, Lu or I, had got it completely wrong and therefore could be mercilessly mocked by the other at various dinner parties. Apparently:

1) I'm an idiot; and
2) Lu meant on a chain around her neck.

That makes much more sense. Furthermore, I have some left-over chain from when I went to B&Q to sort out that issue with the plug for the basin upstairs. Everyone's a winner – well, actually I'm dead when Lu takes on this new piece of jewellery, but you know what I mean. More importantly, I'm not mental.

And what of my other possessions? I don't really have anything else of real value or worth that's mine. I am not saying that I live in a hut with a mud floor and a single tin mug hanging from the corrugated iron roof. It's just that anything I've got is kind of Lu's as well. So (as an example) the most valuable thing bought in recent years is our sofa, purchased from our joint account, which is primarily filled up by my salary. It seems a little petty to leave directions for Lu to be able to keep the sofa. Also, not so romantic for me to say whilst alive:

"Come on, let's curl up together on my sofa."

It implies that we have formalised arrangements for Lu to use it, in a legally drawn-up licence. Quite naturally (being a lawyer) I would have drawn it up and obviously Lu would have had to receive her own independent legal advice. This is standard practice. Whilst the Sofa Licence would, of course, be a concise document, proper protections would need to be built in – I take my work seriously after all. She would be responsible for any damage she causes, fair wear and tear excluded (I'm not an ogre!). The 'Non-Owning Sitter's Covenants' may prove tricky to negotiate. In particular, under the negative covenants, I would insist on a whole section dealing with the prohibition on picking feet whilst I'm eating a take-away.

Second Neuro Assessment – Preparation

This follow-up to the initial assessment testing happens a good few months after the operation and, to be quite frank, I'm nervous about it. To show how worried I am, I have been revising, and my father offered to get me a private tutor. The 'revision' involves me sitting in a pub or restaurant with Lu who makes a variety of different facial expressions at me covering the full range of human emotions. I then shout out "smiling" or "not smiling" after each expression to the bemusement of the waiters and other punters. If Lu has had too much wine this gets tricky. Anyway, it is just like being back at kindergarten, particularly if Lu hides behind the menu whilst deciding upon and practising the next expression. She then sticks her head over the top of the menu and I give it my best shot. It would be more dignified for me if she didn't shout "Peekaboo!" each time. On evenings where I get more than half right I get an extra bedtime story.

As I get better and better at this I do not just stick to smiling or not smiling but have moved on to some pretty advanced stuff, and now actually describe the expression, whatever it may be, not just limiting myself to happy and sad. "Existential angst", I might cry, for example, "Mild incredulity" or "Bemused indifference". I'm getting good at this and will soon be A-level standard. The expression that I most commonly get is Lu miming to me that I have a piece of sushi seaweed stuck between my front teeth, but that is cheating because she uses her thumbnail to assist her expression of disgust.

Second Neuro Assessment

I was ready for it this time, with my tutoring and hours of revision.

Looking at this critically, some of the questions were a bit off-piste and I struggled to see the rationale. In one section I was shown a picture and I had to say what the picture was of. This is like what I used to do with my daughter a couple of years ago before she grew out of it. Anyway, I was waiting for the standard Child stuff: apple, orange, pirate, dinosaur. If they do it alphabetically (which is the standard) then I have a pretty good idea what 'X' is going to be without even looking at the picture. It is always X-ray or Xylophone. Always. I think it would be overly harsh to try us with a picture of a Xenophobe so soon after a brain op. What pictures did I get?

1) *Monocle.* I knew it – most people do. But hardly an everyday word.

2) *Sextant.* Did not know that, but then it is rare that I use one. Maybe I should and it would help me get out of Highgate Woods. It also demonstrates clearly when they last updated this test. The latest version should, of course, replace this with Satnav.

3) *Centaur.* Seriously? Slightly unfair unless you live in Greek mythological times.

Who came up with these ridiculous and obscure objects? It must have been a 'graduate' from the Cannabis Trial.

I was then asked to define certain words, for example "Encumbrance". Now I generally hate to get all sniffy about things, particularly with people who are trying to help me. But "Encumbrance" is a legal term and therefore this is my territory. I gave the perfect answer:

"A third party right, interest in or claim attaching to an asset or item of property potentially affecting its marketability or transferability, and frequently used as a form of security."

The psychologist looked at me blankly and blinked a bit. I insisted that he update his answer book. Possibly they include a word for each profession or job to see if the patient recalls the basic language required for his or her work. The Monocle could be a hang-up from when the test was used for opticians in Victorian times, and Sextant for the navigators. Yet these neuro-psychologists and their damned tests have missed the most obvious questions:

"Prior to the operation did you have any superpowers and to what extent have they been affected by the operation and subsequent chemo and radiotherapy?"

My preparation paid off and my results were promising: apparently in terms of being clever, I am now around the 50th percentile – a massive improvement since the last test done soon after the operation. The neuro-psychologist was most impressed. 50th percentile? I don't want to sound arrogant, but I hoped to be above average on most mental functions that don't involve finding my way out of a wood. So why was the psychologist so pleased? Apparently the last test had placed me on the 99th percentile. That's 99 per cent down from the top, i.e., if there were 100 people in a room including me, I would probably be the stupidest. Or on average I would be the stupidest. Or the probability of me being the thickest person in the room is 99 per cent. I don't actually know which one of these, if any, is correct. (Don't forget though, I used to be on the 99th percentile, so do not expect too much from me.)

For future tests, they should use words that are going to be relevant to the patient. Since diagnosis I have not encountered a single Monocle, Sextant or Centaur. They should change these to:

1) Pills.
2) Sick bags (I use a brand of bags that has no little air holes that could cause drips).
3) More pills.
4) Laxatives (not in pill form, as this is covered by the previous category).
5) High Fibre cereal.

Holidays

As a result of my illness our two-week holiday driving to the South of France had to be cancelled. Our holiday has become another casualty of this horrible disease. Instead, we changed it to five days in a forest-based holiday centre. It does have a continental feel to the place but mainly because most of the people seem to bloody cycle on the right.

My brain works in strange ways now it has been carved up like a Sunday roast, although I always had a slightly odd perspective on things. Let me give you an example of how I now 'tick'. In the main pool area of the holiday centre I noticed that there were approximately 100 people (as a guesstimate). Let us imagine that a terrorist cell stormed the pool and forced everyone to line up against the wall in strict order of intelligence, with the cleverest at the deep end and the stupidest where the shallow end begins. (They would order hostages in this way because, obviously, the brightest people would need a closer eye kept on them as their collective genius could be planning a counter-attack whilst at the dim end of the line, the individuals probably struggled just getting their swimming costumes on and working the lockers.) Let us further suppose that everyone in the pool knows their precise level of intelligence in absolute terms and also the identity of the person immediately cleverer and immediately thicker than them in the room. Here is my point: a few months ago I would have been the person at the end of the line at the very shallowest bit of the pool, looking up to the deep end in awe of those boffins. Whilst everyone else (except the genius at the extreme other end) would have a buddy on either side of them (one slightly cleverer and one slightly thicker) I would only have one friend and he or she would be on the cleverer side of me. I would be the only one without a thick friend to look down upon. This troubles me enormously. In fact, next time I go there I am going to bring my Cambridge degree certificate (laminated of course – us Cambridge graduates are intelligent enough to realise the recklessness of bringing our degree certificates in to a swimming pool complex in an un-laminated form) to demonstrate that my place at the Thick End is temporary only and induced by illness. I can absolutely guarantee that I would be the only person in the "Below 1.5 Metres Depth" section of the line to be holding a laminated Oxbridge degree certificate. I think you will find that those terrorists have seriously misjudged me and should devote at least one henchman solely for the purpose of keeping an eye on me. I am plotting the escape right now and it's damn clever. There is no telling what I could do with my law degree including the module in Roman Law.

I must give credit to the holiday centre, though, for their ingenious locker system. It must be everyone's worst nightmare to come out of the pool to find their locker broken into and someone nearby using their dry towel and special shampoo. I say "worst nightmare" in the sense of it meaning "quite annoying indeed". Anyway, the point is that you do not want people in your locker, hence the 'lock' bit of the name of what are basically numbered cupboards. Everyone wears their key on a wrist or ankle band created on the fair assumption that Speedos do not come with zipped pockets. Normally at swimming pools the key or band comes with the locker number on, as only someone of Stephen Hawking's mental calibre can remember a two- or three-digit number for half an hour when there is so much distracting fun to be had. Taking myself as an example, in my current state I can remember a single digit number for up to thirty seconds if there are no distractions at all and if I constantly repeat the number out loud. So what happens if the band falls off? Someone could work out your locker from the number and, before you know it, they will be lathering up with your favourite anti-dandruff shampoo and then shoving your clean and dry towel into the depths of their rear crevice before dragging it back and forth in that sweeping motion. You would be lucky indeed to escape with just a wet towel and you would instead be likely to take your favourite towel back home from holiday with all of those happy holiday memories represented by someone else's skid-marks on it. Anyway, this is the genius bit; the wrist/ankle bands have no numbers on but contain a chip which you can hold up against a special chip-reading machine and this tells you your locker number. Told you it was clever. However, this is not a totally fool-proof system: if the band fell off or was stolen I suppose the towel and shampoo thief could do this scanning thing too in a dramatic identity theft. So it needs to come with a retina scan as well.

With my pear-brain I inevitably forgot my number in the short walk from the chip-reading machine to my locker. The solution here is to have a mobile chip-reading machine that you can wheel to your locker with you, constantly reminding yourself of the number on the way.

This got me thinking generally about my tumour-induced memory loss. Why not have a chip like this inserted into my forehead. In the house and dotted around London would be chip-reading machines which, when I touch my forehead to them, would immediately tell me:

1) What I am currently doing (other than head-butting an innocent machine);

2) What I should actually be doing, where I should be doing it and how I get there;

3) Which of my children I am currently looking after and responsible for;

4) What I have recently done wrong and who I should be apologising to (top five only);

5) Which laxative I take next and when; and

6) How long it is until nap time.

More Chemotherapy

Having successfully survived this disease so far, my reward is more chemotherapy and it's grim. The doctors have doubled my dose and I have four little red and white pills in the morning five days a month.

The first morning was the worst. Four chemo tablets, a fry-up at the café round the corner and then … up it all came. This is actually very traumatic for me, particularly as I suffer from emetophobia (an irrational fear of vomiting). In fact I haven't vomited (prior to that day) for over twenty years. I guess it's like riding a bike and the technique came straight back to me. I found the process relatively easy, in fact, effortless – it was all done for me by my stomach and diaphragm. These two parts of my body had the process totally in hand. Now I am completely cured of my emetophobia: being sick before the chemo has passed through my stomach means I haven't had the chance to absorb these supposedly cancer-busting (and therefore life-saving) chemicals thus depriving me of essential treatment. I am still terrified of puking. However, this previously illogical anxiety over vomiting has therefore become a totally rational fear. Phobia cured.

Return to Holiday Centre

I accept it is not very original to go on holiday twice to the same place within the space of a few months. However, there is something there for each of us in our family and it seems to work for us as an escape for a few days. I also like the idea of travelling less than an hour to get there. It also meant that the brilliant Alan could join us. We did all the usual stuff but one particular afternoon stood out. It happened when Thea (my five year old daughter) and I went swimming together. Of all the pools in the complex, Thea chose the wave pool as it has a big shallow end, fountains that spring up and, of course, waves.

We were playing a wonderful game where Thea was the mummy and I was the baby. With the aid of the buoyancy provided by the water, Thea would carry me around in her arms like her baby and then, after a few moments, would 'accidentally' drop me on my head and I would dutifully sink beneath the waves. Where did she learn such parenting skills? Let's not explore that question in too much depth. Admittedly I did drop my younger son, Sacha, when he was a baby. He was in a Moses basket and in scooping it up, I only managed to grab one of the handles, so that he rolled out banging his head on the floor. So there is history of this in the family. Although in my defence: firstly this was an accident and secondly I did it once not over and over again over the course of an hour. Anyway, Thea and I were having loads of fun splashing in the waves and playing 'negligent parent' when suddenly an incident occurred. The lifeguards all sprang into action and shouted:

"Out of the pool! Straight away please!"

People were not taking a huge amount of notice and the lifeguards seemed to be losing some of their authority, so I decided to help. Let me explain. First of all, I have this trait. Whenever I see a mix of the very humourless together with the potential to be ridiculous (particularly where toilet humour is involved) I step forward, roll up my sleeves (metaphorically of course – my trunks don't have sleeves) and get stuck in. I cannot help myself – it just happens. I joined in with the lifeguards but changed the script slightly:

"Out of the pool now please. There's a shark!"

People looked at me with a variety of expressions but, strangely, followed my orders more readily than the lifeguards'. Do we really classify acts such as this as "lying" when the motive is to save lives? OK it was not a shark, but clearly there must be some danger to necessitate this "emergency evacuation" (an apt expression as it turned out). It could not be a rehearsal – everyone (apart from me) looked much too serious. It was the real thing. At this point in proceedings one of the lifeguards (perhaps the chief one) drowned me out by shouting one of my favourite quotes of all time:

"It's not a shark! It's a poo!!"

The fellow lifeguards joined in to make a chorus out of this new saying. Me being me, I could not leave things like that. I have to get involved. Failure to do so would be a crime against toilet humour. I said to the lifeguard:

"I am really quite concerned here, are you sure you are properly trained to do this?"

Once I had started, I carried on:

"My recommendation is that one lifeguard climbs up one of those giant chair-ladders or ladder-chairs (I do not know their correct name as only lifeguards and tennis umpires use them. Apart from 20 seconds pretending to be a lifeguard, I have experience of neither profession). From this view point the elevated lifeguard could act as spotter and direct the others with the benefit of a better vantage point."

Meanwhile, I was still basking in the fact that I had made a dozen lifeguards all shout

"It's not a shark, it's a poo."

With hindsight, I think that I may have been overly harsh on the lifeguards as a poo would definitely get me out of the water quicker. Anyway, my lifeguard reassured me that they already had a spotter and that they had all been properly trained to deal with this exact situation. To them this was routine – all in a day's work. Furthermore, there was no health risk whatsoever to the pool users. The chemicals dealt with that. I am not sure I believed the lifeguards last point, but did not want to get into an argument, when my opponent had a full blown crisis on their hands. My killer argument (which I never got the chance to make) is: If the chemicals can so easily and effectively deal with the situation without any chance of hazard to bathers, why not leave the poo alone? Let it bob around freely in the waves. At this point, one must not forget that this is a *wave* pool. In other words they were trying to recreate the feeling and ambience of the sea and a beach. When mimicking the sea, what could be more authentic than a turd floating past you? In fact, they should throw in a used condom and a dead seagull to really give it that seaside flavour.

Then followed my favourite part of the whole holiday. Another lifeguard elbowed his way to the 'shore' carrying a giant net in one hand. He was a skinny guy with national health glasses but he looked like he knew what he was doing. So viewing the situation from the shore, he puffed out his chest, nodded to his colleagues, pushed his glasses further up his nose and then, without a moment's thought for his own safety, in he dived carrying his giant turd-net. This was "Baywatch Bedfordshire". I waited a short while to see the dramatic "rescue" but started to get cold and bored. I do also wonder if the poo had simply dissolved and the chlorine sorted out the resulting solution ("solution" in the chemistry sense). In the end, the lifeguards claimed it was a false alarm and in fact there was never any poo (or shark). Furthermore, there were far fewer people and therefore much more room in the pool after that, for the rest of the day.

This kind of thing must happen all the time and kids (and adults) must constantly be peeing in the water. My idea would be to have a giant chrome handle on one of the walls. Whenever a poo scare happens, an official simply yanks the handle down ninety degrees and the entire pool flushes itself away down a big hole which opens in the middle. To mask any smells, little yellow pine smelling blocks could be scattered about (more for reassurance than hygiene) and any solids or puddles that don't get sucked down or that accidentally leave traces on people, could be wiped away by tissue paper which is kept on a handy spool attached to the wall. With all these brilliant ideas, this centre ought to hire me.

Advice

If you are unlucky enough to find yourself in a situation similar to mine, you may wish to bear in mind some of this advice.

No one knows how long they've got. It's just that my time line is shorter than most other 44-year-olds. Whether you are like me or "normal", just take each day one at a time and extract as much as you can from it.

If the end is in sight, don't just wind everything down; start something completely new. Set your sights high – very high! For example: I have recently considered applying to do some voluntary work for an organisation such as Excellence in Education (EIE). Education is a topic close to my heart (having been a teacher), I'm quite good in a public-facing role and want to do some voluntary work, perhaps as this organisation's Information Officer (known as the IO) or a similar role.

I've also (since childhood) had a desire to run a tiny farm, just for a year or so, as a kind of hobby (rather than as a commercial venture) and as a break in my career pattern. A chance to "recharge the batteries". I find fruit-picking very wholesome and I love animals. It also must be therapeutic to create your produce straight from the ground. A childhood dream never fulfilled. Maybe I'd first have to put in the hours serving in fast-food outlets to raise more money, just on a part-time basis, to keep some cash coming in whilst the farm project is reaching fruition, and to support me when doing voluntary work. If you think that I have not set my sights particularly high here and that this career path looks random or contrived, I would draw your attention to my future CV and, in particular, the "Employment and Experience" section which would be (and I say this without exaggeration) the greatest one in the history of mankind, ever. It would simply read:

- McDonald's
    - Had a farm
        - EIE IO

Here's another idea: phone up the London Borough of Barnet or whoever your council is. Try to get put through to the most obscure person (by category) you can think of. So when you finally get through to the switchboard, you should say something like:

"I would like to speak with the person who has ultimate responsibility for individual council collections for the disposal and recycling of prickly intruder hedge clippings."

After speaking with fifteen different people, all trying to get rid of you as quickly as possible, suddenly death is no longer something to fear. Instead it is seen as a welcome relief.

Wills

Having put it off for months because I did not want to face the finality of it, Lu and I have just made arrangements to sort out and update our wills. If you have never done this before, you will be unsurprised to hear that it is a depressing exercise. Not simply because it is all about your death. The process is not just about your death but quite a few deaths. What one has to do is imagine all the people closest to you in your whole life and whom you love the most. Then you play out every possible scenario of them (and you) dying in every conceivable order and at every age. This could be turned into a fantastic family game to be played after Christmas lunch. You have put away the turkey carcass and finished the Christmas pudding.

"So who wants to play 'Who Dies Next'?"

The various will conversations go something like this:

"So let us suppose that they don't live to their eighties but they die horribly and simultaneously in a car crash in which the deeds to the house get destroyed in the resulting fire. Little X would, unfortunately, be in the back of the car. He/she miraculously survives the crash but in everyone's confused and battered state, in stumbling out of the car they fail to notice the meteor heading towards them. Meanwhile ABC and XYZ [not their real names] were meant to be the guardians of our children. Now I am having second thoughts bearing in mind their propensity to find misfortune wherever they go, including being attacked by gorillas on that safari I am about to imagine. If they cannot avoid such disasters (particularly as I am now

about to send them a text warning them) are they really fit to bring up our children who will still be totally traumatised by our deaths caused by us both falling into the walrus enclosure at London Zoo shortly after the tube of fish paste unexpectedly exploded on us? The will doesn't cover that scenario, does it?"

My Superpowers

As I have mentioned I have not always been this unlucky. In fact I was born with various "gifts" which, up to this point in time, I had kept rather quiet about for obvious reasons. After all Peter Parker and Clark Kent both valued and clung on to their human form anonymity as long as possible to avoid being pestered by fans, the Press and the like.

My "gifts" are admittedly less impressive than the conventional ones of, say, being able to fly, running at the speed of a racing car, being able to look through walls and sending burning laser beams out of my eyes. However, I would not part with my powers for the World. Unfortunately, they are not incredibly useful and do not include the ability to defeat brain cancer. Anyway, time to "fess up" and finally go public:

Superpower 1

I have a super-human sense of smell. I have never known any human to come close to my ability and, in the animal world, I rank myself a little below a bloodhound. Let me give you some examples:

1) In an environment where I know everybody fairly well (e.g. my old place of work with a headcount of about 70) I can tell, by smell alone, the identity of the last person (or sometimes last couple of people) to have used the lift, assuming no one has gone in and broken wind in between the occupation of the lift and me "sampling".

2) If I stand on the edge of a pavement with my eyes shut or with me blindfolded and a car drives past with at least

one window open on my side, I can tell whether or not that car is a mini-cab. Mini-cabs have a very specific smell being a cocktail of old vomit, stale cigarette smoke and air fresheners in the form of those little pine tree shaped pieces of card hanging from the rear-view mirror. You can tell it's a mini cab (thus confirming my claim) by the extra aerial at the back and the official "sticker" confirming that, despite their appearance, the driver is not as dodgy as he may seem.

3) I have a party trick. I must know everyone involved pretty well for it to work. An item of clothing is given to me belonging to one of the guests (a jumper or something, nothing smutty), again whilst I am blindfolded. I can usually (or often) tell the owner by the smell alone.

So Superpower 1 is a super-human sense of smell.

Whilst this is the most straightforward of my "gifts" it is the one people are least likely to believe. The comment I most frequently get is that surely people just smell of their perfume / after-shave / deodorant / soap and therefore I am doing nothing more than demonstrating that, as the cosmetic companies claim, their products really are new and unique. No, no, no! Every person has a unique smell. This interacts with the smelly products they are wearing to produce a slightly altered unique smell (or in some cases, altered dramatically into a suffocating, gag-inducing artificial fragrance). But their smell is still in there. Applying a visual analogy to my olfactory point, it is the equivalent of my doubters saying:

"How could you possibly recognise him as John? He was wearing a T-shirt and trousers!"

As you might expect, some people have a particularly good smell, some a bad smell and others may have a bland smell of nothing at all. Interestingly, there is no correlation whatsoever between how nice their smell is and how visually attractive they are. Some very attractive women have bad smells (and I do not necessarily mean body odour, just a smell that is not pleasing to the nose) and some random person of either gender may smell pretty good. Sometimes a person has a bad smell but it is impossible to identify the particular offensive pong in question – it is just a case that the smell of that person does not work. In the same way, people with nothing particularly "wrong" with them can look unattractive. They can have all the right bits in all the right places, no hideous growths or parts missing, but put it all together and the look does not work. Maybe the eyes are too close together, the face has an unpleasant asymmetry to it or you simply do not like the big bushy moustache that she is growing.

If categorising, there are two particularly bad smells a person can have that can be identified:

1) The "bed smell". The overpowering notes to come across are of unchanged sweaty bed linen and stale skin flakes. This is the smell equivalent to hair's visual "bed head". Gross. Don't you people shower in the mornings?

2) A particular perfume smell. I say this in generic terms partly to avoid legal problems and partly because there is a particular perfume (or a couple of them), whose name

I do not know, which is totally over-powering, heady, sickly and gets you right in the back of the throat. It can smell more flowery than a bee's fart and I cannot bear it, particularly in restaurants. I will move tables to avoid such people (embarrassing if the perfume / aftershave wearer is part of my dining group). The smell can be so strong and unpleasant that it can severely hinder the effectiveness of Superpower 3 (see below). Again, using visual clothing analogies (which I think is the best way of explaining), wearing such perfume is the equivalent of taking someone out to dinner in the following scenario: I am wearing a dash of my favourite aftershave, a small amount of deodorant and emit the remnant smell of my shower gel (sartorial equivalence of jeans and a casual shirt). My companion would be wearing this awful perfume or an aftershave of similar effect in huge quantities (sartorial equivalence of chubby bloke in a mankini). I consider such fragrances in such quantities rude. It is like them saying:

"I don't care about your smell or the taste and smell of your food; my smell must prevail."

It is like shouting over someone whenever they open their mouth to speak. It also has a strong bearing on my emetophobia (hence the need to swap tables). What's more you cannot say anything to the person in question. You may think it is like telling someone they have bad breath or body odour. No, it is much worse because they have *chosen* to wear it. So my message to them would have to be:

"Not only do you smell terrible but you have willingly elected to do so. Please do not wear that perfume ever again in my presence. It puts me off my food and may affect my future memories of what we both intend to eat – I will just remember me eating pot pourri and you eating flowery toilet freshener. I hope I have not offended you – I don't mean to. In the nicest possible way it's just that I feel it may trigger an episode of emetophobia. Oh what does that mean? Nothing rude about you at all. It just means that your choice of perfume is inducing an irrational fear of vomiting in me."

I think inclusion of the word "irrational" stops this being an offensive comment. In other words (I would explain)

"My fear of puking because of your perfume is really my issue not yours."

Who could possibly be offended by this when I have laid the blame squarely at my own feet?

Superpower 2

Several times in my life (at least three times) I have been hit in the face by bats (as mentioned earlier, I mean "bats" as in the flying mammal not the wooden implement used in cricket). To further clarify, not "hit" as in punched. "Hit" as in a fly hitting a windscreen on a fast travelling vehicle (but thankfully, without "bursting" in the process). In other words, whilst on holiday visiting, say, a cave or an old stately home, bats have flown splat into my face. Not a brush past or a glancing blow. A full on, comedy-style splat into my head with flappy wing skin and little claws everywhere round my head. In my considered opinion these were accidents on the part of the bats in question, not acts of aggression nor misplaced and ill-performed displays of affection. I can tell by the expression. Animals (certainly mammals) do have facial expressions and on none of these occasions have the bats in question been snarling or giving me the evil eye. The bats' expression on every occasion (and I could not have got a closer look) is very very clear: total surprise (matching my own expression) but mixed with a look of idiocy, and embarrassment clearly meaning:

"Doh, what am I like!! Better get this sonar looked at during my next service."

My only possible explanation is that my body density is precisely that which renders my body "transparent" to bats' sonar squeaks. I have even asked a vet what could cause this but she was as in the dark as I was (if you will excuse the pun) possibly because half of the participants in each collision were human and not animal, and she is a vet. A crash between, say, a flying squirrel and a camel she could have diagnosed and understood.

So Superpower 2 is that I am undetectable to bats.

Superpower 3
This is my least useful superpower. In addition to the fact I have yet to find a single benefit or use for this power, it inevitably gets me into trouble. It is of academic interest only.

I can remember what I ate and what the person accompanying me ate at a restaurant if the meal in question occurred at any time in about the last ten years. However, there is the catch: Whilst I can remember in detail what both of us ate (it does not work so well with big groups) at a particular eatery, I cannot remember the identity of my companion. So why do I get into trouble with such a seemingly harmless (and useless) power? Typically I would go out to a familiar restaurant with Lu, and can state in immense detail what we ate last time we were there, a few years back. The detail extends to the type of bread or olives provided at the beginning right up to the type of chocolate or mint presented at the end with the bill. The problem is that I will proclaim with some confidence that the last time we were there Lu had a bowl of mixed olives and sour dough bread, followed by the Dover sole in dill sauce with pudding of a shared Eton mess garnished with extra raspberries. Lu well and truly takes the wind out of my sails by insisting she has never been to that restaurant before. Yet I am certain that Superpower 3 is fully functioning and produces data which is error-free. Then the penny drops: I have been there before. The recollection of the food is completely one hundred percent accurate (down to the little pieces of lemon mixed in with the olives) yet it was not Lu I went with but an ex-girlfriend. In other words, as Lu points out (and which is very difficult to refute), I pay far more attention to my food and my companion's food (which I inevitably finish, or at least sample) than I do to the evening's company. My feeble defence is that, being at a restaurant (which, after all, is all about food), it is natural to focus primarily on this aspect, if for no other reason than out of respect to the chef. I am sure people (regular people, not superheroes like me) can see a film with a friend, remember the plot years later but not which friend they took. So what difference and why am I in trouble? It does happen the other way round where Lu was with me for the first meal. Then I can remember Lu as my companion for the evening mainly because I will clearly remember only getting half of a dessert (and how crestfallen I felt when Lu asked the waiter/waitress for that second spoon). In Lu's defence, she claims that she cannot eat a whole dessert and she is not as greedy as me. My response:

*"I **can** eat a whole dessert. I can also eat one and a half desserts, so order your own."*

As with many aspects of my life, Gary makes things a whole lot easier. He is a creature of habit if ever there was one. We nearly always go for curry and he always has the same thing: popadom and chutney starter, lamb bhuna, pilau rice, plain paratha and (if he is allowed) cauliflower bhaji. I say "if allowed" because his long-suffering wife claims it gives him terrible wind. I believe her: most foods do this. If it is Chinese he will have crispy fried beef, rice, duck rolls and will start off with a soup that looks like a certain body fluid.

Superpower 3 is therefore a photographic memory when it comes to food eaten out.

I have always wished to put these powers to good use in the fight against evil. I am not exactly sure how they could be utilised and, to date, the Police have shown no interest whatsoever in harnessing my skills. Most criminals are put away through forensic evidence or visual witness identification rather than smell. Most villains' lairs (outside of Scooby Doo cartoons) are not accessed via caves filled with bats to raise the alarm. And the restaurant meal thing is of no use at all. In fact, people are generally unimpressed by this power as there is no way of verifying my proclamation.

Anyway, "Meal Memory Smelly Batman" (as my alter ego is known) is still working on a costume and, perhaps, a better name. I have suggested to the East Finchley constabulary that they install a light that shines a beam on the underside of clouds with my logo on. I am still working on the design of the sign although it contains images of:

1) A bat.

2) A face dominated by a handsome and prominent nose - image 1) of course being superimposed with image 2).

3) A thought bubble with a picture of a meal in it.

If my powers are required they shine this into the sky. Much better than simply phoning my mobile. I quite like the idea of a cape as part of this outfit although its flappiness could easily inhibit the stealth associated with Superpower 2.

The good news is that Pear seems to have acquired none of my Superpowers, and all three powers appear to have chosen to reside in "rest of me" in preference to Pear. In the interests of complete fairness I would point out that, since my operation, I have not had a chance to test Superpower 2 owing to a real paucity of bats in the East Finchley area. Perhaps it has been a bad winter for bats. Alternatively, perhaps I am completely oblivious to the fact that I am constantly being dive-bombed by bats who, in mockery, detect me perfectly and pull away at the last second like an overly reckless stunt pilot who has drunk too much coffee.

This has got me worried and I am starting to doubt myself. Just the other day I was reminiscing about a curry I had with Gary in February 2005 and, wait for it, I could not remember his starter. This sent me into a tailspin. Everything started to unravel! I even phoned the restaurant but they do not keep till receipts that far back.

Hang on, I got it! He just had popadoms and chutneys. What threw me was that he did have an onion bhaji but he chose to have this as a side dish. Schoolboy error on my part. Anyway, panic over. I still believe I retain all three of my special gifts.

Funerals

Since my diagnosis there have been a couple of funerals that I could have attended. People I knew of rather than knew so my attendance was not vital. Just as well because on each occasion I felt unable to go. It would just disturb me too much watching the coffin being lowered in and covered with earth. Hearing those thuds of mud hitting wood and me standing there thinking:

"That will be me next." and

"I wonder what my funeral will be like. Will it be like Great Uncle Fred's where everyone was so sad and we then went back to his unoccupied flat afterwards for prayers, a whisky and a bite to eat? Nothing too flashy, just bagels with salmon or egg filling, a bit of herring, a few bowls laid out of hand cooked sea salt and balsamic vinegar crisps, some Spanish pimento-filled Queen olives, a dozen or so egg and onion bridge rolls, chocolate marble cake and a bowl of Quality Street from which somebody had picked out all the purple ones (which are my favourite). I can't remember who was there though – must have been blotted out by the intensity of my grief."

In fact I have my cemetery plot booked for me. It is a double one (my companion-to-be being Lu of course). This does freak me out somewhat and cannot be that easy for Lu. Anyway, I will keep it nice for her whilst I wait (hopefully a very long time) for her arrival. Having shared a bed with Lu for nearly 20 years I do have some concerns. I do not want to spend the rest of eternity feeling a bit chilly because she has surreptitiously nicked all the soil.

Bucket List

One of the first things I did following my diagnosis was to finalise my Bucket List. Bearing in mind that I was not sure I would actually get out of hospital, some of these items do not appear very ambitious. The list goes something like this:

1) Take my middle child, Sacha, for tandoori lamb chops at the curry house round the corner. Easy, and done almost straight away.

2) Take my elder son, Jonah, to see Godzilla (the film). Done as I have already mentioned.

3) Five weeks backpacking around Cambodia and Laos with Lu. Just ain't going to happen.

4) An anniversary night away. Called in some child-sitting favours and we had a couple of nights in Barcelona visiting my lovely friend Mary-Ann.

5) A badly behaved Chinese meal with Gary, Carl and Kim. We have done this several times although we are now running out of Chinese Restaurants in North London as we cannot return to any previously visited for obvious reasons.

6) The 2014 Punt Trip. Done. Details have already been mentioned.

7) A trip to Amsterdam with my brothers, Martin and Nick. This used to be an annual occurrence, but with kids and responsibilities acquired by all three of us, these trips stopped a while back. Anyway, they were fantastic

whilst they lasted and we fully enjoyed the delights this city had to offer. We saw a couple of great shows. Not boring old Cats or Phantom but an alternative circus type act involving the most peculiar one-man (in fact woman) game of table-tennis I have ever seen. I had no idea how the scoring worked but she was going to win anyway being the only participant. Interestingly this sole participant seemed totally unperturbed by the absence of a table, which I had previously considered absolutely fundamental to the game. The finale was a bottle of Coke drunk in the most unconventional manner you can imagine. It did look like thirsty work though playing all that ping pong.

Before leaving Amsterdam we decided to try to visit somewhere cultural. On one occasion we went to the Van Gogh museum. I even listened to the CD audio guide whilst going round so I would have clever things to impress people with at dinner parties when I got back. For some reason, upon our return, not a single person believed we went to the Van Gogh Museum. Even when I made it clear this was not the *only* thing we did, parents, relatives and friends thought this cultural bit was entirely fictitious and we were not given the benefit of the doubt. I am certainly not going to bother doing that kind of cultural thing this time round if nobody believes me.

Competition for Food

Having each meal with my brothers whilst in Amsterdam brought back memories of the competition for food between the three of us when growing up, and how such competition was despised by my parents who therefore subjected us to various rules:

Rule 1: **Don't fight over food**; Self-explanatory really.

Rule 2: **You can't save food**; So eat there and then. Any requests for more food prefaced by "Well last time I didn't have as much [WHATEVER FOOD ITEM WAS] so I get more now" will get short shrift.

Rule 3: **Don't waste food** (particularly meat).

We liked it when we all had a common enemy. The most common of these adversaries was a chain of pizza restaurants, well known for its salad bar. It is very odd that, pretty much the whole time at home, we had salad available on tap, if we could be bothered to open the fridge door and pull it out of the crisper. So if we are normally so indifferent about salad, why does a visit to the pizza restaurant turn the whole family into salad grabbing monsters? It is partly the competition between us and partly the absolute burning desire to get the best possible value for money, even to the extent that we stack the bowl up with foods we do not even like:

"I hate gherkins, but at least these are free."

As well as the greed, why do we all suddenly get so unconventional and weird about the ingredients of our DIY salad?

"Yes I always put croutons on my salads, and also little red crunchy gravelly stuff that looks and tastes like burnt oven scrapings."

If you want to have a side salad at an outlet of this chain, as I am sure you know, the waitress presents you with an empty bowl or plate, depending upon which size you order. You then make your own way to the salad bar which is always located in the space closest to the Gents. For the remainder of this advice, I will assume that one is ordering the small side salad which must be assembled in a smallish bowl given to you. If you order a big salad you are presented with a large plate or equivalent crockery, but this is cheating and shows clear salad grabbing incompetency. Follow this advice on how to get the most salad with a small bowl and one visit to the salad bar and, in just two or three salads (depending upon various factors), your purchase of this book has paid for itself.

The restaurant chain's salad bar has only one rule when it comes to the side salad and in this sense is quite liberal. There is no obligation to eat healthy stuff or combine items that go together. It is completely legitimate to have a lake of blue cheese dressing with a few radishes and beetroot pieces bobbing in it. It is also perfectly legitimate to have 100% croutons although whether you could actually call that a "salad" is questionable. The rule: Only one visit to the salad bar. Just one chance. If you leave the restaurant feeling salad-deficient it is your own fault. The way they phrase the rule is very much to turn it into a challenge. You simply have one small bowl with which to acquire a lifetime's salad and to bankrupt the restaurant chain.

Are you really going to run away from this challenge?

The Salad Thieving Eleven Stage Bowl Technique™ works like this. Before I continue I emphasise that the bowl (small salad size) looks so much smaller than the plate (i.e. big side salad size). You do not need a technique for the big salad plate – there is simply loads of room. Therefore I limit my advice here to the small side salad which must fit into one small, slippery, brown bowl.

You know when you have done well. The Rule says one visit but of course, after a successful trip using The Salad Thieving Eleven Stage Bowl Technique™ you cannot eat out of the actual bowl used – this would cause numerous salad avalanches engulfing you, your companions and neighbouring patrons of the restaurant. However, whilst you cannot use a big plate to harvest the salad, you are allowed one to *decant* the contents of the bowl once your sole visit is complete. So when presented with (after requesting) a large main course-sized dinner plate you carefully place it over the bowl (not that it will be able to touch the rim) invert the plate/bowl combo and stand back. You know it's a good foraging session when the salad collected won't fit onto this giant plate. Instead it cascades over the side in all directions. Sometimes I ask for two large plates just to make my point. Do not forget to save a smug look for those who paid for the big side salad. You may be waist deep in salad, dressing and croutons – more than you can possibly eat, and looking like you fell into a compost heap, but you are victorious.

I am at that point in my life where I want to leave a valuable legacy to society. I think my salad piling technique might be it.

So how is it done? Sit back, pay attention and learn. Here is the The Salad Thieving Eleven Stage Bowl Technique™. Use it wisely:

1) Smear the inside of the bowl with the stickiest dressing – usually blue cheese but sometimes thousand island.

2) At the bottom of the bowl place two large dessert spoons of coleslaw or potato salad or Russian salad. It does not matter which but it must be both dense and sticky. Smear this towards the corner where bottom part of the bowl hits the slopey bit.

3) Take about eight celery sticks (the longest they have) and arrange them evenly round the edge of the bowl, with the bottom end of each firmly rooted in the dense/sticky salad (whatever you chose) sticking upright but lying snug against the slopey bit of the bowl (assisted by the coating of dressing described in 1.) If you have sensibly brought a protractor with you, that is forty five degrees between celery sticks but do not worry if you are a degree or two out or a stick of celery down. Do not miss this step even if you hate celery. The celery more than "pays" for itself in terms of space taken up.

4) Find about four of the biggest and flattest lettuce leaves. Weave these in and out of the celery "girders" leaving as few gaps as possible. Any holes that appear can be patched up with cucumber slices stuck on with further mayonnaise or dressing. Congratulations, you have doubled the size of your bowl! The restaurant manager is now getting nervous, and rightly so.

5) Now in the bottom of your enlarged bowl put in dense salad such as coleslaw, pasta salad, sweetcorn and the like. This is a good opportunity to include items of salad that you actually enjoy eating rather than chosen for their civil engineering properties. No tomatoes though.

6) Carefully fill the rest of the enlarged bowl with ingredients of decreasing density as you ascend. Still no tomatoes.

7) When you think you can fit no more in, carefully coat the entire outside of the mound in blue cheese dressing. Remember you will be standing right next to the Gents. So pop in there and give it just 30 seconds to one minute under the hand drier (not too close as the salad may not yet be structurally sound). Hold around thigh level and make adjustments for any super-high-power driers that may be installed. You want the blue cheese dressing to harden significantly but not lose its stickiness. This is important unless you wish to stop at stage 7 (in which case why not just waste your money on the big plate salad, you quitter!).

8) More salad (such as grated carrot) will now adhere to the outside of your structurally-sound salad mound, potentially increasing its size by up to 20%.

9) Repeat stages 7 and 8 up to three times.

10) Any crevices or gaps should be plugged with croutons (big holes) or sweetcorn kernels (small holes). Ignore any cracks that may be structural at your absolute peril – instead fill these gaps with mayonnaise and croutons.

11) *"But I like cherry tomatoes!"* I hear you cry, my salad grabbing friends. Here is where the lawyer in me comes out. The Rule about one visit must stand – that is Gospel. To break this is cheating and brings about an instant lifetime ban from using the The Salad Thieving Eleven Stage Bowl Technique™. It is that serious. But nowhere in the restaurant does it say that the one visit must result in all salad being *contained* within the boundaries of the bowl or (grrr) the plate. Cherry tomatoes (with a dab of thousand island assistance) should be balanced round the rim, held in place by the dressing and, importantly, your thumbs. I have checked the menu carefully and this is not prohibited. There is definitely no requirement whatsoever for the selected item of salad to have its centre of gravity directly above any part of the bowl.

There you go – enough salad to feed a small Ghanaian village for a week.

Morocco

Despite not being on the bucket list, the kindness of my parents (i.e. babysitting for four days on the trot), meant that Lu and I got to Marrakesh. We had a fabulous few days there enjoying eating everything in tagine-form and drinking endless cups of sweet mint tea in markets.

The etiquette for pouring mint tea is unexpected. One must hold the teapot so that the distance fallen by the mint tea is the maximum possible, making it nice and bubbly, but without splashing the person pouring too much or others in the vicinity. So not dissimilar to English urinal etiquette.

The Future

My current predicament and medicalisation affects every single aspect of my life. It is very tricky getting away from it even for a short period of time and my outlook on life has completely changed. There is no such thing as a normal headache any more. Any pain to any part of my head is a matter of concern. Completely binary. No "just a headache for me". In fact nothing falls between:

1) Too mild to actually detect, and
2) Aaaaaggghhhh, it's come back!

One particularly hard thing to deal with is the question I get asked several times a day from genuinely well-meaning people: "So how are you?". It is different to the normal "How are you", asked by way of a greeting rather than a literal enquiry into health. But it is different in my case when I am asked this question because:

1) It is a genuine enquiry into my health and not a casual greeting. I know this because
   i) the question starts with the important word "So" which means "I really mean this question. Really, really, really.";
   ii) it is a "real" question and it does not have to be asked at the beginning of the conversation but can be thrown into the chat at any point in time and
   iii) there is huge emphasis given to the word "are" to the extent that that this one syllable word alone can take up to two seconds to say: longer than "so", "how" and "you" combined! The very concerned people can add

further emphasis by including a tonal change half way through the "are": downwards to empathise with my despair; upwards to indicate the optimism we must all cling on to.

2) Despite being a genuine enquiry based on genuine concerns, they do not want a proper answer such as:

"Sit down as this will take twenty five minutes or so. Let me start with my bowel malfunctions and gradually work upwards through my body."

3) My response is totally mood-based. The stock answer is the dead standard:

"Fine thanks, how are you?"

(said in a slightly sing-song voice).

And on bad days:

"I'm dying, you moron. I've already asked you and a "plus one" if you will come to my funeral."

I will have regular scans and, on each occasion, will be right on edge for the couple of weeks beforehand. It is just a waiting game now between me and the tumour. Who is going to blink first?

Birthday

It is my birthday fairly soon. This gives those around me a problem. What do they give me? Sorry to be morbid but there is no point in getting me 'stuff' or 'things' unless they are consumable. The card may be tricky and I can imagine the excruciating conversations in various card shops around North London where the shop attendant says to my friend/family member:

"Is it a special birthday you need a card for?"
"Yes, indeed."
"How lovely. Which birthday is it?"
"His last."
"I don't think we have a card for that."

They should stock these 'Last Birthday' cards. There must be a market for it. In theory as many should be needed to be produced by the greeting card industry as the 'Welcome to the World/Newborn Baby' cards. In the long term the number should be the same.

My Last birthday card needs to have one of those little rhymes in it. I suggest something like:

> *This very special birthday*
> *You must be elated!*
> *Cos next year you'll be dead*
> *And buried or cremated.*

Today

I am now living how I should have lived up to the point of this disaster. One day at a time getting as much as I can out of every single hour. Living my life simply by placing one foot in front of the other. I do not think too hard about what lies around the corner. However, I also want to leave Lu and my children in the best possible position. Whenever I see my oncologist she does stress that there are survivors, however rare they are. In other words there is a theoretical prospect of my survival but my chances are very slim at best. She says:

"But don't give up! There are survivors!"

Whilst I appreciate the reassurance this is a bit like an in-flight announcement as follows:

"This is the captain speaking. I regret to inform you that all engines have failed and this plane is now in an uncontrolled free-fall into the Indian Ocean just off Somalia. You will therefore, in all likelihood, burn to death, drown, get eaten by sharks or killed by pirates. These options are not necessarily mutually exclusive. However, on the more positive side, in 2009 Bahia Bakaria managed to be the sole survivor after her plane crashed into the ocean. So don't give up! There may be survivors. Meanwhile, the duty free trolley will be passing through the cabin shortly and please buy our charity raffle tickets which supports this month's selected charity 'Feed Foreign Fish' which, ironically, raises money for starving marine life in the Tropics."

Acknowledgements

So many people have helped me medically, socially and generally. Too many to list but I'd like to make a few specific mentions:

- Lewis Thorne: You performed a fantastic operation and (apparently) did not barf whilst chopping up my brain. Well done indeed! You deal with my ridiculous questions e.g. Can I go on water slides? Can I use a Samurai sword in a martial arts class? Shall I buy a new pair of jeans? ("Yes" to each).

- Naomi Fersht: Your manner and technical ability are fantastic. In the unlikely event I get out of this mess, I will miss our regular meetings.

- Eileen Andrews: You are always available, reassuring, knowledgeable, lovely and everything a specialist NHS nurse should be.

- The rest of the NHS team who got me this far: thank you. Boo to private healthcare!

- Gary, Kim and Carl who have kept me uncivilised and sane throughout this ordeal.

- Susanne Worsfold for all her excellent work producing the cover of this book.

- My parents for stepping in every time we have a "personnel crisis" or need some other form of support or help.

- Dad, Martin, Nick, Ros, Richard and Paula: thank you for your thorough proofreading.

- All my other friends and family who have done so much for me. Karen: thanks for your many acts of friendship and keeping a concerned eye on me over the months. Your many texts mean that I never feel forgotten.

- The firm I work for: Pemberton Greenish in Chelsea. I was hit with this illness less than two months after joining them. Yet I was straight away treated like one of the family and looked after well by them. My partners, colleagues and clients have all been great to me.

- Jason: thanks for the steak. Your mention here is payment of my debt (as agreed). Get me a medium-rare rib eye and you can be in any sequel I write.

- Josie: your advice has been so valuable. Thanks for your expert guidance in this project.

- Carl: thanks for all your help and many hours of wise input. You kept going when I started to feel the fatigue. It would not have got over the line without you. Thanks mate!

- Above all, my three adorable children who keep me grounded as well as wonderful Lu. You are with me every step of the journey, supporting me every hour of every day and are extremely tolerant of living with someone with only two-thirds of a brain in their head. Lu, the remainder of my life is devoted to ensuring I leave you in the best possible position (in terms of sorting out the house, spiritually, emotionally, financially and in terms of your memories). I love you more than I can find words to represent. I don't know if you can miss people after you die but I feel I will be missing you for eternity. I hope the royalties from the book are enough for you to have fairly regular sushi nights.

*****

So the end of this book finds me ten months on from Pear discovery, having got through some of the hardest treatments science has devised and still completely in the dark about how much time I have left. Like every other person on this planet, I should take life one step at a time as I can never know what comes next or when it will come.

36040735R00080

Made in the USA
San Bernardino, CA
11 July 2016